GW00859231

The P'ni-El Therapy

Face to Face with G-d

Dr Beverley M Anderson

THE P'NI-EL THERAPY: Face to Face with G-d

Published by Beverley M Anderson

Copyright © 2018 by Beverley M Anderson

All rights reserved

No part of this book may be reproduced or transmitted in any form or by any means, electronic or mechanical, including photocopying, recording, or by any means of information storage and retrieval system without permission in writing from the publisher.

Unless otherwise indicated, all Scripture quotations are taken from the Complete Jewish Bible, Copyright © 1998 and 2016 by David H. Stern. Used by permission. All rights reserved worldwide.

Scripture quotations marked AMP are taken from THE AMPLIFIED BIBLE Old Testament copyright © 1965, 1987 by The Zondervan Corporation. The Amplified New Testament copyright © 1958, 1987 by The Lockman Foundation. Used by permission.

ISBN: 978-0-244-70803-0

Cover photograph: **Beverley M Anderson**

Printed in the United Kingdom

The Man asked him, What is your name? And in shock of realization, whispering he said, Ya'akov, supplanter, schemer, trickster, swindler!

Genesis 32: 27 AMP

Contents

Introduction 8

1. Generational Sin and Iniquity 13
    a. Perversion
    b. Generational Roots
    c. Roots and Fruits
    d. What is Iniquity?
    e. Iniquitous Patterns
    f. The Hidden Strangers
    g. Origins of the Hidden Strangers
    h. Perverted Worship
    i. Primal Origins
    j. Conclusion

2. Tracing Iniquitous Patterns 33
    a. Moving out of G-d's Timing
    b. Wrong Place, Wrong Time
    c. A Four-Generational Iniquitous Pattern
    d. Obey G-d and Starve the Hidden Stranger
    e. Conclusion

3. Iniquitous Traits in a Family 38
    a. Family Traits
    b. The Relationship between Traits and Iniquitous Patterns
    c. Know Your Weaknesses
    d. Familial Spirits
    e. Fault Lines
    f. Familiar Spirits
    g. Family Curses
    h. Spiritual Strongholds

i. Conclusion

4. Confront Sin and Iniquity 49
a. The Seed
b. The Root
c. The Tree
d. Conclusion

5. Spending Time Alone 56
a. Yeshua Spent Regular Time Alone
b. Ya'akov needed to Send Time Alone
c. Ya'akov was Born to Breakthrough
d. Be Kingdom-Minded
e. Family Traits
f. The Guardians of your Oral History
g. Conclusion

6. Your Encounter with G-d 65
a. Ya'akov Returns to the Womb
b. Battle at the Gates
c. Name Change, DNA Change
d. Conclusion

7. Your Encounter with Yeshua 72
a. Prepare to Meet Your G-d
b. Your Illicit Love Affair with the World
c. Fame
d. Money
e. Pleasure
f. Yeshua can Pinpoint the Cause of your Thirst
g. Emotional Restoration
h. Spiritual Restoration
i. Conclusion

8. Teraphim, Family Idols 87
a. The Living Room

b. Imaging
c. Household Images
d. Re-Call, Re-Member and Imitate
e. Conclusion

9. Breaking Down Satanic Altars 97
a. Drug House
b. The Spirit of Bondage
c. Appetites and Cravings
d. Hidden Strangers Revealed
e. Who are the Hidden Strangers?
f. Identify the Hidden Strangers
g. Your Dead Relatives have Influence in your Lives Today
h. The Drug Dealer – Trafficker
i. The Witchdoctor
j. Conclusion

10. Hold on To Your Liberty 112
a. Kingdom Culture
b. Eden – The Environment of G-d's Son
c. An Authentic Union with G-d is achieved in His Son
d. True Freedom in The Messiah
e. Shalom – The Missing Factor
f. Worldly Believers
g. Keep A Check on Yourself
h. Mental Slavery
i. What is a Curse?
j. Identify Curses
k. Mikveh – A Daily Immersion in G-d's Word
l. Hearing G-d's Word in a Three-Dimensional Way
m. Hereditary Curses
n. Voluntary Curses
o. Curses Over Nations
p. Trauma Induced Curses
q. Curses Produced by Our Words

r. Curses that enter through the Doorway of Leadership
s. Choose Blessings or Curses
t. Conclusion

11. The Self-Diagnostic Approach 134

a. Decide to Win the Battle
b. Self-Diagnosis
c. The Prognosis
d. Self-Analysis
e. Cultivate Your Garden
f. The Terms of an Agreement Between G-d and Man
g. Making A Mental Aliyah
h. Identify Your Symptoms
i. The First Step Towards Liberation
j. The Second Step Towards Liberation
k. The Third Step Towards Liberation
l. The Fourth Step Towards Liberation
m. Conclusion

12. Calling Leaders to Freedom 141

a. Self-Diagnosis and Prognosis Sheet
b. Weakness Awareness Sheet
c. Prayer of Repentance Sheet
d. The Prophetic Act
e. Prayer of Protection Sheet
f. Renunciations: The Seven Enemies of Kena'an
g. The Treatment Application Sheet
h. Conclusion

Glossary 146

Author's Contact Details 151

Introduction

The 'Generational Curses' carried in the bloodline of every family on earth, is the real issue of human suffering and pain. It is that hidden *sin principle*, at work in the lives of every human being. These curses entered into the roots of every family because of Adam and Eve's disobedience to G-d's command. Disobedience altered the human genome and caused it to become separated from G-d and separated from His life-giving benefits. Adam and Eve's separation from G-d was evident in the fact that they hid themselves from His presence. However, the deeper issue here, is the change that occurred in their bloodline. Man's rebellion, had caused him to be numbered amongst *'the fallen ones.'* I believe the fallen state of human nature, provided a doorway through which *the fallen angels* could enter and attach themselves to the human bloodline. These fallen angels are the **'Hidden Strangers'** who have become the **'spiritual parents'** or *'familial spirits'* who attached themselves to the bloodlines of the human family. They are the rebellious spirits who are characterized as having *appetites and craving* that cannot be satisfied, and a thirst that cannot be quenched.

I think it would be correct to describe these *rebellious fallen spirits* as the original blood sucking vampires we often see as the fictionalized characters produced by Film Makers of today. They not only **share** the bloodline of a family's life;

through each of its new members, they **transfer** their evil characteristics and personalities. Fallen spirits cannot help but reveal their craving to feed their addiction for sexual immorality, impurity and indecency; involvement with the occult and with drugs; in feuding, fighting, becoming jealous and getting angry; in selfish ambition, factionalism, intrigue and envy; in drunkenness and orgies.[1]

The primary goal of these rebellious fallen spirits is to establish their insatiable appetites and addictive tendencies, in human beings, in order to, steal, kill and destroy the image of G-d in them. The god of the *'olam hazeh* has devised systems that feed the habit created by the *'hidden strangers.'* The Devil's agenda is to keep you in the dark; those who belong to his kingdom are deceived and many who belong to the Kingdom of G-d have been blindsided. The truth is that every family on earth whether rich, poor, free or slave, is in need of G-d's life-giving intervention because **all** suffer from the same sin-diseased bloodline that continues to perpetuate life-threatening dependencies.

Many of you are relying on a world that can only offer treatment for the symptoms of sin and the dependencies it creates, without knowing how to cure **the cause**. This is the reason why the world's answer to treating your pain, is to provide you with an unlimited supply of food, alcohol, prescribed medication and narcotics. Over indulgence

---

[1] Galatians 5: 19-21

quietens the cravings and satisfies the appetite, only temporarily. Whether self-prescriptive or medically prescribed, the world is only able to treat the symptoms. The Greatest Physician is G-d. He is able to heal **the cause** of your symptoms and make you whole. G-d is Omniscient!

Being born again does not guarantee you a trouble-free life. Salvation does not offer you an 'opt-out' clause to life's challenges. The Father rescued you from the dominion of darkness and transferred you into the Kingdom of his dear Son. Because of this, you are the greatest threat to the domain of darkness.[2]

As you embark on The P'ni-El Therapy training course, you will become increasingly aware of the *'rebellious fallen spirits'* attached to your bloodline. Be ready to do battle with them because they will put up a fight to remain in control of your soul (mind, will and emotions). You will also become increasingly aware of the rebellious activities of these *'hidden strangers'* as you begin to learn how to identify the strategies they use to survive in your life.

This teaching course will show you how important it is to *immerse yourself* in G-d's Word of Truth. In order to become fruitful in your ministry, it will be necessary to know *how to* do the following:

---

[2] Colossians 1: 12, 13

- Identify the 'hidden strangers' in your bloodline.
- Identify iniquitous patterns and traits.
- Identify 'generational curses.'
- Confront the roots of sin in your bloodline.
- Expose, call out and renounce demonic influences.
- Unlock traumatic memories of your past and confront them.

This book will help you to identify all major hindrances to your personal, marital and ministerial development. You will be given the tools to close the door on **generational curses** in your life, your marriage, your family and any ministerial positions you may occupy.

There is an established iniquitous pattern related to *an established dictator* who speaks into in your bloodline, demanding that the voices of their thirsts, desires, appetites and cravings be heard and fulfilled. Generations of law breaking in your bloodline have caused you to experience the effects of spiritual traumas that you are unable to understand or articulate. Trauma in the bloodline will prevent you from stepping out in the victory that was won for you on the Messiah's Execution Stake.

From time to time we all need a thorough detox to get rid of poisonous toxins that build-up in our bodies. In order to detox successfully, all unhealthy and unnatural foods will need to be removed from our diet. Our bodies crave foods that contain life, such as fruits and vegetables, however bad eating habits suppress the body's desire to consume life-giving foods. When unhealthy foods are replaced by healthy foods, our bodies react by going into defense mode. Sudden changes can challenge longstanding addictions; that is to send a person's body into crisis and cause symptoms of withdrawal to manifest. The typical symptoms that occur when a person is withdrawing from narcotics or prescription drug dependency, range from agitation, anxiety, sweating, seizures and depression to abdominal cramps, diarrhea, nausea, vomiting, dilated pupils and more. The withdrawal process depends on the type of drug dependency and the length of time drugs were consumed.

This teaching course aims to sensitively probe the inner recesses of your mind, will and emotions, to expose the 'hidden strangers' in your bloodline and help you to identify iniquitous patterns.[3] At the conclusion of this teaching course, you will have found the courage to close the door on generational sin and iniquity in your bloodline. Remember, the battle has already been won.

---

[3] Mishlei (Proverbs) 20: 27

1 Generational Sin and Iniquity

The sins of your ancestors have a great influence on who you are today. Their sins have created weaknesses in your bloodline. As a result, you were born with a susceptibility to the influences of perverted character traits. Your ancestors allowed sin to enter into your bloodline by forsaking G-d's law. Their rebellion caused twisted laws to be established in your bloodline. You inherited a perversion of G-d's law. Your family traditions, culture and belief-systems were established on *twisted laws*. Twisting G-d's law is a perversion of G-d's law.

a. PERVERSION

Perversion gives license for **hidden strangers** to take up residence in your bloodline. You may have noticed that you are *strong-willed* in some areas and *weak-willed* in others. These two extremes may be the workings of the **hidden strangers**, whose purpose is to *instill perversion* until they overtake your bloodline. They are the deviant cohorts whose assignment is to separate you and your descendants from your G-d given purpose. The offspring of Perversion, *weakens your will* to the powers of temptation; they take control of the mind, will and emotions by *opposing* any idea that threatens to usurp their position.

Generational sin in the bloodline occurs when the perversion of G-d's law becomes established throughout the lifetime of one family. This is called First Generational sin and can be passed onto the children of the Second Generation and so on. Susceptibility to certain types of sin becomes stronger in each generation, and each new member is at the mercy of the *hidden strangers* in their bloodline. In other words, when innocent **babies** are born, they *develop a susceptibility* to the generational sins of their bloodline and are defenseless against its temptations. This is what it means to be born *guilty*.

b. GENERATIONAL ROOTS

Since we were all born *guilty*, there will come a time in our lives when we will have to confront *our own sins*. I am talking about the sins of our bloodline. If you were never taught about the importance of dealing with *generational sins*, you may not be able to go any deeper than the fruits they produce in your life. If a generational root is not dealt with, you will be locked into a cycle of asking the Father to forgive you for *a reoccurring sin*. King David became aware of the generational roots of his sin after his affair with Bat-Sheva (Bathsheba). In a song he wrote, King David laments about being confronted by his sins. He admits that he was conceived in sin and born guilty.[4]

---

[4] Tehillim 51

---

c. ROOTS AND FRUITS

Some trees thrive and grow for hundreds and thousands of years because they have a strong, healthy root system. **The life of a tree is in its roots** and its longevity depends on how deep and extensive those roots are. Even when a tree has been chopped down, after a short period of time, new shoots will grow out of the old stub that remains in the ground.

You are part of a family tree that is connected to *generational roots.* Your generational roots are the relatives in your bloodline, past and present. Your bloodline consists of ancestors who have established your tradition, your culture, your spiritual belief and your identity. Your living relatives, particularly the older ones, reinforce established tradition and culture. They seek to retain a revered status of ancestral rights, in order to transfer *hidden strangers of the bloodline*, to the next generation.

You are the inheritor of the plans and purposes of the *hidden strangers*, established by your ancestors. You may not know what their plans were whilst they were alive, however, your bloodline contains their specific rebellion against G-d. Study the tree and you will see that the purpose of the fruit is contained within **the seed**. After the seed is planted in the ground, it produces a root that eventually becomes an underground root system. The **root** therefore, contains the purpose of the **fruit**. Your bloodline and the root system of a tree are similar in function and purpose:

Roots:
- Are unseen (*in the blood as in the earth*)
- Contain life
- Have the ability to reproduce after their own kind

Adam was the first sinner and his sin opened the door to rebellion against G-d's law in your bloodline. Rebellion against G-d's law is in the bloodline of every human being born into this world.[5] Each family bloodline is sinful and can be identified as having specific satanic character traits in varying degrees. Some families are known criminals and others carry a distinct air of Pride and Snootiness. Learning how to identify *generational roots* within your life, will put you on the road to liberating your current and future generations from enslavement to the *hidden strangers* who have overrun your bloodline.

d. WHAT IS INIQUITY?

Inherited illnesses such as Hypertension or Cancer, can reinforce a weakness or susceptibility to these diseases in a family line. Similarly, unrepentant sin can leave a spiritual weakness towards that sin in a family line. This is called '**Iniquity**.' The definition of *iniquity* is a **generational deviation** from G-d's proper path. Iniquity is **a strong craving** toward a certain type of sin that entered the bloodline of a family; its iniquitous patterns are established

---

[5] Romans 5: 12

---

in the traditions of future generations e.g., *suicide, acts of violence etc.* A family craving toward a certain type of sin, produces an addiction in an individual, that is reinforced by an established system of belief and encoded in their DNA. The root of addiction to certain types of sins, originally introduced by an ancestor, becomes biologically embedded; a revelation now being understood by genome analysis.

The Hebrew word for **Iniquity** is called *havvah* (No. 1942) and means:

> *'root: 'hava' [1933],* **to breathe, to exist**
> **craving, coveting,** *desire, mischief*
> *mischievous, naughtiness,* **perverse thing,**
> *very wicked.'*[6]

Knowingly or unknowingly, your forefathers permitted **fallen rebellious spirits** to take charge of your bloodline. These rebellious spirits are the *hidden strangers* and *spiritual parents* that you have never met. They are more acquainted with your bloodline than you are! The very substance of who you are is intertwined in the inheritance that your forefathers have left you. Your ancestors left you an inheritance that is cursed, because *they decided to deviate* from

---

[6] Strong J., 1822-1894, *The New Strong's Complete Dictionary of Bible Words,* Thomas Nelson Publisher, Nashville, Tennessee, U.S.A., 1996, p. 352

G-d's ordained path for their lives.[7] Eikhah (Lamentations) chapter five and verse seven says, '*Our ancestors sinned and no longer exist; we bear* <u>*the weight*</u> *of **their guilt**.*' The Amplified Version of the same scripture text says,'*...we have borne **their iniquities**.*'

e. INIQUITOUS PATTERNS

Iniquitous patterns are observable traits and actions that come from *evil spirits*, attached to the bloodline of a generation. A reliable example of iniquitous acts and tendencies, can be accurately observed through *a three-generational bloodline*. If not dealt with, iniquitous patterns will prevent you from moving in G-d's timing. Iniquitous patterns are the character traits associated with the **hidden strangers**, mentioned earlier; they are the *evil spirits* who exist in the bloodline.

f. THE HIDDEN STRANGERS

The reason that these *hidden strangers* cannot be easily detected, is because they are spirit. Hidden strangers are the evil spirits who lie undetected in the bloodline for generations. Evil spirits do not have a physical body; they are invisible to the eye. Evil spirits attach themselves to the bloodlines of living families. Most of us have no idea how or why these **hidden strangers** share our bloodline.

---

[7] Sh'mot (Exodus) 20: 4, 5

However, the New Birth experience will cause you to become aware of these hidden strangers, especially when you begin to be transformed by the renewing of your mind. The Word of G-d is the fire that will test and prove your mind. His Truth will reveal the hidden strangers and shatter strongholds in the mind of every believer.[8]

g. ORIGINS OF THE HIDDEN STRANGERS

As a member of the Messianic Community of Believers, you would never want to be told that there are evil spirits attached to your bloodline. Yeshua dealt with all this on the Execution Stake, right? Yes, He did. However, as long as we live in the *'olam hazeh*, we have to contend with *our old nature*. In his letter to the Messianic Community of Believers in Rome, the Emissary Sha'ul shares with them, his own internal struggles with **"the hidden strangers"** of his old nature:

> [7] Therefore, what are we to say? That the *Torah* is sinful? Heaven forbid! Rather, the function of the *Torah* was that without it, I would not have known what sin is. For example, I would not have become conscious of what greed is if the *Torah* had not said, **"Thou shalt not covet."** [8] But sin, seizing the opportunity afforded by the commandment, worked in me *all kinds of evil desires* – for apart from the *Torah*, sin is dead. [9] I was once alive outside the framework of *Torah*. But **when the commandment really encountered me, sin sprang to life,** [10] and I died. The commandment that

---

[8] Yirmeyahu 23: 29; Romans 12: 1, 2.

was intended to bring me life was found to be bringing me death! [11] **For sin, seizing the opportunity afforded by the commandment,** deceived me; and through the commandment, sin killed me. [12] So the *Torah* is holy; that is, the commandment is holy, just and good. [13] Then did something good become for me the source of death? Heaven forbid! Rather, **it was sin working death in me through something good,** so that **sin might be clearly exposed as sin,** so that sin through the commandment might come to be experienced as sinful beyond measure. [14] For we know that the *Torah* is of the Spirit; but as for me, I am bound to the old nature, sold to sin as a slave. [15] **I don't understand my own behavior – I don't do what I want to do; instead, I do the very thing I hate!** [16] Now if I am doing what *I don't want to do,* I am agreeing that the *Torah* is good. [17] But now it is no longer "the real me" doing it, but *the sin housed inside me.* [18] For I know that *there is nothing good housed inside me – that is, inside my old nature.* I can want what is good but I can't do it! [19] For I don't do the good I want; instead, **the evil that I don't want is what I do!** [20] But if I am doing what "the real me" doesn't want, it is no longer "the real me" doing it but the sin housed inside me. [21] So I find it to be the rule, a kind of perverse "*torah,*" that although I want to do what is good, evil is right there with me! [22] For in my inner self I completely agree with God's *Torah;* [23] but in my various parts, I see **a different "*torah,*"** one that battles with the *Torah* in my mind and makes me a prisoner of sin's "*torah,*" which is operating in my various parts. [24] What a miserable creature I am! Who will rescue me from this body bound for death? [25] Thanks be to God [he will]! – through Yeshua the Messiah, our Lord! To sum up: with my mind, I am a slave of God's *Torah;* but **with my old nature, I am a slave of sin's "*torah.***

Romans 7: 7 - 25

Sha'ul became aware of the *evil desires* of the hidden stranger of greed that was at work in his bloodline, when the *Torah* said, **"Thou shalt not covet."** The hidden strangers will reveal themselves whenever they feel threatened with eviction. The Apostle Sha'ul became conscious of their opposition to the *Torah* when his hidden strangers began to object to specific commandments given. The evil desires of greed, for example, manifested in Sha'ul, to let him know that they are in allegiance with the perverse "*torah*" (law).

When the sons of G-d (fallen angels) saw that the daughters of men were attractive, they had intercourse with them because they intended to have children by them. The fallen Angels committed a grave sin in the eyes of the *El 'Elyon*, because they violated the daughters of men by joining themselves to them. As a result, *the daughters of men gave birth to giants*, who are **part spirit and part flesh**. Because they were born part human, they were assigned to share the human bloodline as *evil spirits*. An explanation is given in the following excerpt, taken from 'The Book of Enoch:'

> XV. 3. Wherefore have ye left the high, holy, and eternal heaven, and lain with women, and defiled yourselves with the daughters of men and taken to yourselves wives, and done like the children of the earth, and begotten giants (as your) sons. 4. And though ye were holy, spiritual, living the eternal life, you have defiled yourselves with **the blood of women**, and have begotten (children) with **the blood of flesh**, and, **as the children** of men, have lusted after flesh and blood as those also do who die and perish. 5. Therefore I have given them wives also that they might impregnate

them, and beget children by them, that thus nothing might be wanting to them on earth. 6. But you were [formerly] spiritual, living the eternal life, and immortal for all generations of the world. 7. And therefore I have not appointed wives for you; for as for the spiritual ones of the heaven, in heaven is their dwelling. 8. And now, **the giants, who are produced from the spirits and flesh, shall be called evil spirits upon the earth, and on the earth shall be their dwelling.** 9. Evil spirits have proceeded from their bodies; because they are born from men, [and] from the holy Watchers is their beginning and **primal origin**; they shall be evil spirits on earth, and evil spirits shall they be called. 10. As for the spirits of heaven, in heaven shall be their dwelling, but as for the **spirits of the earth** which were **born upon the earth**, on the earth shall be their dwelling. 11. And the spirits of the giants *afflict, oppress, destroy, attack, do battle, and work destruction on the earth, and cause trouble*: **they take no food**, but nevertheless **hunger and thirst**, and **cause offences**. 12. And these spirits shall rise up against the children of men and against the women, because *they have proceeded from them*.[9]

The Watchers (sons of G-d) produced children with 'the blood of flesh.' These spirits who were born upon the earth have a hunger and a thirst for that which is not food, they afflict, oppress and destroy. These evil spirits have a hunger and thirst to be *mischievous* and the blood of men and women provide the energy they need to function. These are the children known as evil spirits. Their primal origin relates to

[9] R H Charles, *The Book of Enoch*, Dover Publications, Inc., Mineola, New York, 11501, USA, 2007, pp. 42-43

the spiritual Watchers who fell from heaven in the days of **Jared**. The hidden strangers are licensed to dwell in the spiritual darkness attached to the principle of sin in man.

h. PERVERTED WORSHIP

At a point in eternity past, Lucifer, the Guardian K'ruv was anointed and elevated above those within his own rank. His elevation brought him into closer proximity to G-d and His Throne. Lucifer failed 'the Submission test' because his pride blinded him to see that his 'Promotion' was related to his submission to G-d.

Let us consider another factor that will shed light on the reason why Lucifer was tested. Lucifer's elevation indicated that G-d drew him into a deeper level of relationship with Him.[10] This tells me that Lucifer's promotion, was also about G-d's desire to entrust him with *deeper truths* and untold mysteries. As you begin to grow in your relationship with G-d, He will test your relationship with Him. He will reveal secrets that you will not be permitted to disclose.

The significance of *the relationship test with G-d*, will elevate you to the position of 'rule and dominion.' G-d desires to share His mysteries with you. More importantly, 'Can you handle the mysteries that He is about to reveal to you? You

---

[10] Yechezk'el 28:14

see, the sharing of these intimate details is specifically about 'trust', which is the territory to be conquered, wherever there has been a promotion. Another point that deserves a mention here, is that G-d will answer your questions and share His secrets with you, when you decide to enter into *the secret place* with him.

At G-d's Throne, Lucifer developed a deeper level of union with G-d. Lucifer was *a high-ranking son of G-d, on the level of an angel*, whose relationship began to blossom into a type of Father-son union, where he was permitted to see some of the mysteries of G-d. If this were not true, Lucifer would not have been able to pervert the principles of G-d's Kingdom and use them to build his own.

Lucifer used the mysteries he gleaned from G-d's Kingdom, as a weapon of rebellion and destruction, through perversion. G-d did not give Lucifer the permission to share secrets of His Kingdom. However, Lucifer compromised his right standing with G-d and brought violation to a third of the holy Watchers in Heaven, by revealing secrets that they were not permitted to know. Knowing these secrets caused them to move out of their positions.

G-d shares secrets with those in whom He has an established relationship of trust. <u>If G-d has not given you the release to reveal what He showed you in secret, keep it confidential!</u> You need to know that by revealing G-d's mystery, prematurely, to someone else; may cause them harm.[11] Knowing *how to* keep the mysteries that G-d chose to share with you is to know *the meaning of covenant.* Lucifer was the first angel to enter into *a fallen state* because he was the first sinner. He *took his eyes off G-d* and began to *gaze at his own splendor* and beauty. **Self-deification** produced *iniquity*; the sin first found in Lucifer.[12] The Two Principles upon which Worship is established is Climax and Ecstasy (Labour and Shalom).

At a point in eternity past, Lucifer was elevated above those within his own rank, to occupy the highest angelic position at G-d's Throne. His promotion brought him into G-d's *rest.* Lucifer *received secrets* whilst in a state of *contemplative union* with G-d. Lucifer revealed some of those intimate secrets with a third of the angels in heaven. He would have approached the *chief angels* who had charge over their *hundreds, fifties* and *tens.* In the Book of Enoch, these chief angels were called **Watchers**:

> VI-XI. *The Fall of the Angels: the Demoralisation of Mankind: the Intercession of the Angels on behalf of Mankind. The Dooms pronounced by God on the Angels: the Messianic Kingdom (a Noah fragment).*

---

[11] 2 Corinthians 12: 1-10

[12] Yesha'yahu (Isaiah) 14: 12 – 14; Yechezk'el (Ezekiel) 28: 12 - 18

VI. 1. And it came to pass when the children of men had multiplied that in those days were born unto them beautiful and comely daughters. 2. And the angels, the children of heaven, saw and lusted after them, and said to one another: 'Come, let us choose us wives from among the children of men and beget us children.' 3. And **Semjâzâ**, who was their leader, said unto them: 'I fear ye will not indeed agree to do this deed, and I alone shall have to pay the penalty of a great sin.' 4. And they all answered him and said: 'Let us all swear an oath, and all bind ourselves by **mutual imprecations** not to abandon this plan but to do this thing.' 5. Then swear they all together and bound themselves by **mutual imprecations** upon it. 6. And they were all two hundred; who descended [in the days] of **Jared** on the summit of Mount Hermon, and they called it Mount Hermon, because they had sworn and bound themselves by mutual imprecations upon it. 7. And these are the names of their leaders: Sêmîazâz, their leader, Arâkîba, Ramêêl, Kôkabîêl, Tâmîêl, Râmîêl, Dânêl, Ezêqêêl, Barâqîjâl, Asâêl, Armârôs, Batârêl, Anânêl, Zaqîêl, Samsâpêêl, Satarêl, Tûrêl, Jômjâêl, **Sariêl**. 8. These are their chiefs of tens.[13]

It is clear from the text above, that *Semjâzâ* was given the responsibility to lead his associates (a band of angels) to swear an oath that they would all pay the penalty for the great sin that they were about to commit. Not to say that they hadn't already committed the sin because *they lusted* after the daughters of men.[14]

---

[13] R H Charles, *The Book of Enoch*, pp. 34-35

[14] Mattityahu 5: 28

However, *Semjâzâ's* associates bound themselves to an oath made by **mutual imprecations**. Together *they called down curses and invoked evil*. In other words, they all stood on Mount Hermon and made a request to their Master (the Devil), to inflict evil curses on the children of men, *through the sexual act they were about to commit*. The assignment given to *Semjâzâ* and his associates was to produce children with the daughters of men through *perverted worship*. This was how the hidden strangers initially laid claim to your bloodline.

The name *Semjâzâ* (Shemyaza) means "the (or my) name has seen" or "he sees the name."[15] In other words, he recognizes the lineage. Through the act of Perverted Worship, the Watchers defiled themselves by having sexual relations with the daughters of men. This perverted union served to magnify the darkness that had already existed in the human genome, through Adam's disobedience. The daughters of men, were taught the various secret arts by these fallen Watchers:

> VII. 1. And all the others together with them took unto themselves wives, and each chose for himself one, and they began to go in unto them and to defile themselves with them, and they taught them charms and enchantments, and the cutting of roots, and made them acquainted with plants. 2. And they became pregnant, and they bare great giants, whose height was **three hundred ells**: 3. Who consumed all

---

[15] https://en.m.wikipedia.org/wiki/Samyaza

the acquisitions of men. And when men could no longer sustain them, 4. The giants turned against them and devoured mankind. 5. And they began to sin against birds, and beasts, and reptiles, and fish, and to devour one another's flesh and drink the blood. 6. Then the earth laid accusation against the lawless ones. VIII. 1. And **Azâzêl** taught men to make swords, and knives, and shields, and breastplates, and made known to them the metals (of the earth) and the art of working them, and bracelets, and ornaments, and the use of antimony, and the beautifying of the eyelids, and all kinds of costly stones, and all colouring tinctures. 2. And there arose much godlessness, and they committed fornication, and they were led astray, and became corrupt in all their ways. 3. **Semjâzâ** taught enchantments, and root cuttings, **Armârôs** the resolving of enchantments, **Barâqîjâl**, (taught) astrology, **Kôkabêl** the constellation, **Ezêqêêl the knowledge of the clouds**, (**Araqiêl** the signs of the earth, **Shamsiêl** the signs of the sun), and **Sariêl** the course of the moon. 4. And as men perished, they cried, and their cry went up to heaven ...

XI. 6. Thou seest what **Azâzêl** hath done, who hath taught all unrighteousness on earth and revealed the eternal secrets which were (preserved) in heaven, which men were striving to **learn**: 7. And **Semjâzâ**, to whom Thou hast given authority to bear rule over his associates. 8. And they have gone to the daughters of men upon the earth, and have slept with the women, and have defiled themselves, and **revealed to them** all kinds of sins. 9. And the women have borne giants, and the whole earth has thereby been filled with the blood of unrighteousness. 10. And now, behold, the souls of those who have died are crying and making their suit to the gates of heaven, and their lamentations have ascended: and cannot cease because of the lawless deeds which are wrought on the earth.[16]

i. PRIMAL ORIGINS

The primal origins of the hidden strangers who have attached themselves to the bloodlines of humanity, are related to the Watchers who came down from their heavenly abode and defiled themselves with the women on earth. All the original secrets that were taught to the daughters of men in the ancient world, have become the bedrock of life in the Twenty First Century. The relatives of the Watchers have become *the sophisticated hidden strangers* who have been perfecting their hidden agenda in the bloodline of countless generations. Knowing the names and functions belonging to a few of *the fallen Angels* will be helpful when closing the door to generational curses in your bloodline:

Table 1: **SOME FALLEN ANGELS: NAMES AND FUNCTIONS**

1.	**Jeqon:**	*the one who led astray [all] the sons of G-d, and brought them down to earth, and led them astray through the daughters of men.*
2.	**Asbeel:**	*he imparted to the holy sons of G-d evil counsel, and led them astray so that they defiled their bodies with the daughters of men.*
3.	**Gadreel:**	*he showed the children of men all the blows of death, and he led astray Eve, and showed [the weapons of death to the sons of men] the shield and the coat of mail, and the sword for battle, and all the weapons of death to the children of men.*

---

[16] R H Charles, The Book of Enoch, pp. 35-36

4.	Penemue:	*he taught the children of men the bitter and the sweet, and he taught them all the secrets of their wisdom. And he instructed mankind in writing with ink and with paper, and thereby many sinned from eternity to eternity and until this day. For men were not created for such a purpose, to give confirmation to their good faith with pen and ink.*
5.	Kasdeja:	*he showed the children of men all the wicked smitings of spirits and demons, and the smitings of the embryo in the womb, that it may pass away, and [the smitings of the soul] the bites of the serpent, and the smitings which befall through the noontide heat, the son of the serpent named* **Taba'et.**
6.	Azâzêl:	*taught men to make swords, and knives, and shields, and breastplates, and made known to them the metals (of the earth) and the art of working them, and bracelets, and ornaments, and the use of antimony, and the beautifying of the eyelids, and all kinds of costly stones, and all colouring tinctures.*
7.	Semjâzâ:	*taught enchantments, and root-cuttings.*
8.	Armârôs:	*taught the resolving of enchantments.*
9.	Barâqîjâl:	*taught astrology.*
10.	Kôkabêl:	*taught the constellations.*
11.	Ezêqêêl:	*the knowledge of the clouds.*
12.	Araqiêl:	*the signs of the earth.*
13.	Shamsiêl:	*the signs of the sun.*
14.	Sariêl:	*the course of the moon.*

j. CONCLUSION

Semjâzâ and his associates, performed **a Satanic Ritual Ceremony** on the top of Mount Hermon. Their meeting was the *spiritual initiation of the daughters of men*, through whom they planned to establish World Domination. *Semjaza* and his associates performed **the first Satanic Worship Ritual,** which required covenants to be made. *Binding themselves together by Mutual Imprecations,* they prepared the fallen Watchers to become the medium through which Satan impregnated the daughters of men with his evil sperm. *Semjâzâ* and his associates made an altar on Mount Hermon and bound themselves in Mutual Imprecations. They lifted up their voices *in unison* and invoked all manner of evil curses that came upon the Adamite Race, through the sexual act they were about to commit.

Semjâzâ and his associates **were consumed with lust** during their Satanic ceremony on the top of Mount Hermon. They *invoked their evil incantations* until it reached the point of climax. **When their craving and lust for the daughters of men had reached its critical point,** *Semjaza* and his associates went in and *defiled themselves* with the daughters of men. *The daughters of men were not innocent;* they too, indulged themselves in this unlawful act of perversion. As a result of this ungodly union, the daughters of men gave birth to children fathered by the Watchers.

We do not know all the names and functions of the Watchers who defiled themselves with the daughters of men. The Book of Enoch however, provides the names belonging to a few of the Watchers who *opened the door* to sexual perversion.

*I suggest that knowing the names of the chief Watchers who committed these **acts of sexual perversion** can be of some benefit; especially when closing the door to generational curses in your bloodline.*

Table 2: **Name of Semjâzâ and his associates**

1.	Semjâzâ (Leader)	11.	Armârôs
2.	Arâkîba	12.	Batarel
3.	Râmêêl	13.	Ananel
4.	Kôkabîêl	14.	Zaqiel
5.	Tâmîêl	15.	Samsapeel
6.	Râmîêl	16.	Satarel
7.	Dânêl	17.	Turel
8.	Ezêqêêl	18.	Jomjael
9.	Barâqîjâl	19.	**Sariêl**
10.	Asâêl		

2 *Tracing Iniquitous Patterns*

Sin entered our world through one individual. This means that although you did not violate a direct command, as Adam did, you inherited sin. When you came into this world, you inherited the sin nature and its consequence, which is death.[17] The Bible tells us that human beings have to die once, but after this comes judgment.[18]

If you were never taught, as a believer in Yeshua, that you will have to contend with *generational sin and iniquity*, you may not be able to recognize iniquitous patterns in your own bloodline. Having taught on this subject for a number of years now, I've had the privilege of witnessing many individuals come to the realization that they are *carriers of the iniquitous patterns* in their bloodlines. When the truth dawned on them, they were free.

Acknowledging that you carry the iniquitous patterns of your family bloodline, is the first step towards liberating your generation. In order to arrive at **the recognition stage**, **you must first be taught** what an iniquitous pattern is, and how to identify it in your life.

---

[17] Romans 5: 12, 13
[18] Messianic Jews 9: 27

G-d described David as *a man after His own heart* because *he knew how to touch G-d's heart*. David was a multi-gifted individual, who understood how to thoroughly please G-d in worship. However, David had to confront the iniquitous pattern, that threatened to compromise a fundamental tenet of kingship in the nation of Isra'el.

King David came face to face with Rachav, his Great, Great Grandmother. Rachav (Rahab) was responsible for opening the door to iniquitous patterns in his bloodline because she was a prostitute.[19]

a.   MOVING OUT OF G-D'S TIMING

Iniquitous patterns will move you out of G-d's appointed timing for your ministerial assignments. An iniquitous pattern imbedded in King David's bloodline surfaced at a time when *kings go forth to battle*. All leaders must pass a test that will either be the making or breaking of them.

G-d described David as being *a man after His own heart* because David knew how to be **transparent in worship**. King David was known in the courts of Heaven for the way in which he worshiped G-d, which is why G-d tested him in the area of worship.

---

[19] Y'hoshua 2; 6: 22-25; Mattityahu 1: 5-6

G-d will allow you to be tested in an area where you show the most strength or competency, in order to expose an iniquitous pattern that threatens to remove you from an appointment with your destiny.

> [1] In the spring, at **the time when kings go out to war**, David sent out Yo'av, his servants who were with him and all Isra'el. They ravaged the people of 'Amon and laid siege to Rabbah. But David stayed in Yerushalayim.
>
> **Sh'mu'el Bet** (2 Samuel) **11: 1**

As a king, it was necessary for David to join forces with the other kings, at the time appointed for kings to go to war. Failing to fulfil an apostolic assignment, left David *vulnerable* to **a four-generational iniquitous pattern**. Iniquitous patterns look for opportunities to usurp G-d's authority in your life, particularly when you are in a position of authority.

b. WRONG PLACE WRONG TIME

David became a target for the enemy's plan of destruction, because he was **in the wrong place at the wrong time**. An adulterous union with Bat-Sheva (Bathsheba) ensued, as a result of David's decision to stay behind. The manifestation of David's sin and iniquity, was the loss of his child and a portion of his inheritance. <u>Being in the wrong place at the wrong time, may leave you vulnerable at a critical point in your ministry, and alter the direction of your leadership.</u>

c. A FOUR-GENERATIONAL INIQUITOUS PATTERN

David was related to a four-generational bloodline that had a well-established iniquitous pattern. If David had remained focused on his Apostolic Assignment, he would have been able to overthrow the four-generational stronghold established by Rachav (Rahab), who was a prostitute from Yericho (Jericho).

Table 3: **The Four- Generational Bloodline of King David**

Great, Great Grandparents	Great Grandparents	Grandfather	Father	Son
Salmon & Rachav	**Bo'az & Rut**	**'Oved**	**Yishai**	**David**

The unlawful, rebellious spirits attached to our bloodlines, have established purposes, intentions and cravings. Their ongoing agenda to oppose G-d's Truth, is revealed in our everyday lives through habits that are related to iniquitous patterns. The Hidden Strangers in your bloodline, will wait until you are in *a position of great influence* before they reveal their identity.

d. OBEY G-D AND STARVE THE HIDDEN STRANGER

Obedience to the covenant you made with G-d, will *starve* the hidden strangers in your life and *weaken* the iniquitous patterns related to them. G-d requires your obedience because He wants you and your generation to be free from the hidden strangers in your bloodline. G-d wants you to walk in the fullness of your calling. An iniquitous pattern can be annihilated in the third and fourth generation of those who love to keep G-d's commandments. The Satanic Agenda within the bloodline of the Old Nature, will hold on to all living relatives of a bloodline. The hidden strangers can become particularly aggressive in their attempts to regain a foothold in generational bloodlines that revere G-d.

A hidden stranger will lay dormant for three generations within the bloodline of a person who carries a great anointing to lead, just like David. Promotion in ministry sends out a red alert to the hidden stranger, informing him that his presence is requested. In such cases, Satan will deploy his cohorts to wage war at the gates, in order to prevent total annihilation of iniquitous patterns.

e. CONCLUSION

In conclusion, if iniquitous patterns are not annihilated by the third and fourth generation, they will overrun the bloodline of four generations, to form a godless society. G-d will be forced to remove the iniquitous pattern through judgment, as He did in the Antediluvian World.[20] <u>Sustained **obedience to G-d** will starve rebellion in a three-generational bloodline and overthrow the stronghold of darkness.</u>

---

[20] B'resheet 6: 1-13

3 *Iniquitous Traits in a Family*

The hidden strangers in a family bloodline are the spiritual parents who, occupy darkened areas of a person's life, and hold positions of influence, primarily, through *lack of knowledge*. They not only exist in the dark areas of our lives, they are authorized to dominate and replicate themselves in us. The presence of *the hidden strangers* can be detected by *the way they give expression*. Your sin gave them the license to take possession of your mind, will and emotions; *the three powers* they use to pervert G-d's plan for our lives. Their presence can be identified by the unquenchable thirst they have, to become the destructive element in your lives. These Hidden Strangers have *overindulgent appetites* that gorge themselves on the *'olam hazeh*; their cravings produce addictions that aim to steal, kill and destroy.

Hidden Strangers are related to both human beings and the Watchers who fell from heaven. The *Nephilim* are still Giants in all other aspects today, except in physical stature. Their plans and purposes haven't changed, their intentions haven't changed, their appetites haven't changed, their cravings haven't changed and their traits haven't changed.

a. FAMILY TRAITS

When we talk about Family traits, we are talking about *genetics*. This field of study looks at a bloodline to see which traits or defects have been passed down from one generation to the next. Genetics is the branch of science that looks into physical and behavioural characteristics, including medical conditions inherited.[21] When the Watchers defiled themselves with the daughters of men, *genetic mutation* occurred, which further altered the genetic codification in human beings. These changes were responsible for the rapid development of perversion in the Adamite Race.

Family traits are passed from a parent to their child and from one generation to the next. Traits are like the fruits on a tree and both are fed by their roots. The seed within the fruit carries *the original information* that will replicate an identical copy. The tree is identified by its fruit, and similarly, a family is identified by the traits it displays.

ADONAI described the practices of Yisra'el as being disgusting, detestable and shamefully vile and goes on to cite their spiritual father as being Emori (Amorite), and their mother Hitti (Hittite).[22]   Whilst an interest in family resemblance focuses on your facial features, hair texture or your eye colour; this course will focus on identifying

---

[21] https://www.nhs.uk/conditions/genetics/
[22] Yechezk'el (Ezekiel) 16: 1-5

---

character traits that relate to your spiritual parents. The following table, lists some of the traits that characterizes the nature of sin:

Table 4: **Character Traits of the Sin Nature**

1.	Fear	9.	Fornication
2.	Pride	10.	Idolatry
3.	Poverty	11.	Sickness
4.	Gambling	12.	Gluttony
5.	Adultery	13.	Alcoholism
6.	Insanity	14.	Murder
7.	Divorce	15.	Suicide
8.	Barrenness	16.	Witchcraft

The practices of the flesh originate from the offspring of the fallen Watchers who defiled themselves with the daughters of men. The Watchers introduced evil practices that have been adapted into the cultures and traditions of the nations. National opposition to G-d is evidence of their origin.[23]

b. THE RELATIONSHIP BETWEEN TRAITS AND INIQUITOUS PATTERNS

The practices of the flesh are related to the iniquitous patterns that originate from the root of our sinful nature. The most prominent family trait differentiates one family from

---

[23] Tehillim 2: 1-3

the next. A Strongman tends to be well established in the elders of a family, however, the pattern they produce, is carried in varying degrees, by the other members of the family. Even when family members are separated, each individual becomes the representative of the trait established by the strongman. We all carry our own unique family resemblance whether in facial features, tone of voice, gait, stature or skin colour. Similarly, we each carry the iniquitous patterns, that represent the various character traits of the hidden strangers attached to our bloodline.

c. KNOW YOUR WEAKNESSES

Sometimes an iniquitous pattern may skip a generation, however, *each relative carries a trait that bears resemblance their hidden stranger.* When you register with your local Physician, one of the first things they ask for, is a sample of your blood. They test your blood to see whether you are suffering from **diseases recorded in your family history**. If your tests are clear, you will be checked periodically because *historically, you are susceptible* to contracting **a known disease** in your bloodline. **If you know** the weaknesses in your bloodline, you can begin to **make the necessary changes** to your physical, mental and spiritual way of life.

A *three-generational family* may look like this: The grandmother may be a single parent due to having a daughter out of wedlock. Her daughter, on the other hand, gets married to one man and they have a daughter who appears to be well-adjusted because her parents have a marriage that is well-grounded. In due time their daughter becomes an adult and soon finds that she is experiencing difficulties in being committed to one relationship. The sin committed by the grandmother has skipped a generation and is affecting her granddaughter's life.

Although the Mother raised her daughter within wedlock, the sins of the grandmother (first generation) affected her granddaughter (third generation). The sins of a grandmother created a *weakness* in her granddaughter, which made it difficult for her to keep a covenant relationship.

Generational sin can affect your life because it was initiated by the sins of your ancestors who unleashed the trauma associated with lawbreaking to take control of your bloodline. *If a generational sin is left unchecked it will have devastating effects in subsequent generations;* such as, chronic financial difficulties, chronic alcoholism, chronic perversions, sickness and diseases, barrenness, divorce, accident-prone, premature deaths and mental illness.

Unless you first acknowledge that there are strangers in your house, eject them and close the door; you will not be able to *gain full access to your covenant rights.* In the following Scripture text the Emissary Sha'ul reminds us that Avraham was blessed because *he carried* the promise of G-d's Seed in his loins:

[13] The Messiah redeemed us from the curse pronounced in the *Torah* by becoming cursed on our behalf; for the *Tanakh* says, **"Everyone who hangs from a stake comes under a curse."** [14] Yeshua the Messiah did this so that in union with him the Gentiles might receive the blessing announced to Avraham, so that through trusting and being faithful, we might receive what was promised, namely, the Spirit.

Galatians 3: 13, 14

d. FAMILIAL SPIRITS

What is a Familial Spirit? A Familial spirit is a spirit that is attached to the bloodline of a family. This spirit is likely to be assigned to the most influential and well respected member of a family. Their agenda is to actively perpetuate revolt against G-d in the genealogical bloodline of their forefather, the Watchers. A Familial spirit is like a guardian who uses his influence to ensure that the original plan for world dominion is kept alive in every family.

Familial spirits are responsible for establishing iniquitous patterns in an individual, their family, their extended families and their whole generation. Familial spirits remain hidden in order to keep a firm grip on their position of power. Iniquitous patterns in a family is established on *desecration, infringement, outrage, assault* and *lust for power*. They aim to corrupt your bloodline, so that you will never be able to find your true direction in life.

e. FAULT LINES

Familial spirits create weaknesses in the bloodlines of the families to which they were originally assigned. They established the fault lines and are responsible for the maintenance of those faults lines. They multiply themselves within the bloodline of a living family by adopting and initiating every offspring into their dark world.

f. FAMILIAR SPIRIT

A **Familiar** spirit should not be confused with *a Familial spirit*. Familial spirits operate within family bloodlines, whilst **Familiar spirits** are **conjured up**, to assist *mediums* and *sorcerers* who have asked the familiar spirit for information about people who are no longer living. Many people today pay Mediums and Spiritualists good money in exchange for messages from their 'dead relatives.' Others who claim to be 'Prophets' will deceive you into believing that they are hearing from G-d, when they are really fraternizing with a Familiar spirit.

> [1] Dear friends, **don't trust every spirit**. On the contrary, test the spirits to see whether they are from God; because many false prophets have gone out into the world. [2] Here is how you recognize the Spirit of God: every spirit which acknowledges that Yeshua the Messiah came as a human being is from God, [3] and every spirit which does not acknowledge Yeshua is not from God – in fact, this is the spirit of the Anti-Messiah. You have heard that he is coming. Well, he's here now, in the world already!

4 You, children, are from God and have overcome the false prophets, because he who is in you is greater than he who is in the world. 5 They are from the world; therefore, they speak from the world's viewpoint; and the world listens to them.

6 We are from God. Whoever knows God listens to us; whoever is not from God doesn't listen to us. This is how we distinguish the Spirit of truth from the spirit of error.

1 Yochanan 4: 1-6

Both the *Familial* and the *Familiar* spirits work together to perpetuate Deception. Familiar spirits speak on behalf of the Familial spirits attached to the bloodline, in order to reinforce their systems of belief in living relatives.[24]

g. FAMILY CURSES

Generational sin produces family curses. A curse causes *sorrow of the heart* and gives demonic spirits the legal right to enter into a family, in order to continue their evil practices.

> 'Family curses are reoccurring problems that steal, kill and destroy. You need to learn how to break a curse. Scripture is clear God visits the iniquity of the fathers upon the children up to the third and fourth generation (Exodus 20:5).

---

[24] D'varim (Deuteronomy) 18: 10-12

Curses don't visit your family without cause. When someone up the family tree gives spirits the right to visit because of iniquity, they come looking for a reason to mess up your life.'[25]

h. SPIRITUAL STRONGHOLDS

'*A spiritual stronghold is a mind-set impregnated with hopelessness that leads us to accept as unchangeable, situations that we know are contrary to the will of God ... Strongholds are built in the believer's mind by Satan so he can manipulate behavior without being detected.*'[26]

Strongholds in the mind are produced by accepting a lie. Hasatan, the father of lies became the god of this world, and has set up systems that are founded upon lies.[27] Those who do not know the truth, can be easily persuaded to believe the lies that come from this world. The devil is cunning in presenting his lie as truth – once you accept his lie, you will be drawn into a deception that will form strongholds in your mind. The structure that defends the devil is; the lies and deception of the mind.

---

[25] http://www.jonasclark.com/battling-generational-family-curse/

[26] http://adopt.transformourworld.org/en/mentoring/strongholds

[27] 2 Corinthians 4: 4

Some of the strongholds that affect whole families are: *superstition, mocking G-d, opposing the Torah, unbelief, idolatry, legalism, humanism, religion, antisemitism* and so on. These thought processes can become deeply entrenched in the minds of a three-generational bloodline.

Until and unless strongholds are torn down, you will experience difficulties in fulfilling the purpose to which you were called. Once a negative stronghold is established, it will give demons the legal right to be protected in the bloodline. In his book, *The Three Battlegrounds*, Francis Frangipane reveals 'how to identify hidden strongholds:'

> *'If you want to identify the hidden strongholds in your life, you need only survey the attitudes in your heart. Every area in your thinking that glistens with hope in God is an area which is being liberated by Christ. But **any system of thinking that does not have hope, which feels hopeless, is a stronghold which must be pulled down.**'*[28]

Only the Word of G-d can *deconstruct* and *dismantle* the evil strongholds of your mind. Applying the Truth of G-d's Word to your mind, will expose lies and deception.[29] **Your mind must be renewed and transformed** before you will be

---

[28] Frances Frangipane, *The Three Battlegrounds*, New Wine Press, PO Box 17, Chichester, West Sussex PO20 6YB, England, 1994, p. 43

[29] Messianic Jews (Hebrews) 4: 12

able to distinguish between the Truth and the lie.[30] When **Truth** becomes the stronghold in your mind, it will translate into attitudes and actions that show forth G-d's light.

> [3] For although we do live in the world, we do not wage war in a worldly way; [4] because the weapons we use to wage war are not worldly. On the contrary, they have God's power for demolishing strongholds. We demolish arguments [5] and every arrogance that raises itself up against the knowledge of God; we take every thought captive and make it obey the Messiah. [6] And when you have become completely obedient, then we will be ready to punish every act of disobedience.

2 Corinthians 10: 3-6

i. CONCLUSION

I encourage you to begin to identify the iniquities that are afflicting your family. Look at the iniquitous patterns that operate in your own life and in the members of your extended family. Try to remember statements made about certain family members such as: *"Jackie has a bad temper just like her Aunt,"* or *"Trevor really has an eye for pretty girls, but I remember someone telling me that Daddy also had an eye for a pretty girl, at his age."*

---

[30] Romans 12: 1, 2

4 Confront Sin and Iniquity

There isn't a person in the world today, who wouldn't find it difficult to acknowledge, confront or confess their own sin and iniquity. Knowing that you've made unconscious or willful mistakes in life, doesn't give you a warm fuzzy feeling inside. Our transgressions leave us feeling guilty and condemned. Our ancestor's transgressions, have caused a rebelliousness that affect the choices we make today. The lawbreaking committed by our forefathers is *the reason* we experience inexplicable habits. Why? Because **we are the carriers of their cravings, their appetite and their traditions**.

All decisions made when our ancestors were living, have had great influence on the decisions we make today. Our ancestors have been the silent partners and influencers behind many of the decisions we make in our lives. Since we know the difference between right and wrong, however, we are held accountable before G-d for the sins we've committed.

a. THE SEED

In order to confront our own sin and the sins in our bloodline, we must leave our old life behind. Avram (Abram), as he was known before his departure from Ur of the Kasdim, was a well-respected dignitary amongst his family and townsmen. However, one day, *ADONAI* urged Avram to leave everything that he knew behind. G-d planned to make His own nation and create a righteous bloodline by using Avram as His seed. This is why G-d chose to make Avram into a great nation.

> [1] Now *ADONAI* said to Avram, "Get yourself out of your country, away from your kinsmen and away from your father's house, and go to the land that I will show you. [2] I will make of you a great nation, I will bless you, and I will make your name great; and you are to be a blessing. [3] I will bless those who bless you, but I will curse anyone who curses you; and by you all the families of the earth will be blessed."

B'resheet (Genesis) 12: 1-3

Avram was commanded to *turn his back on* the country of his birth, his relatives and his father's house. In order to receive G-d's blessing to be made into a great nation, and be a blessing to the nations, Avram was required to **leave**:

1. **His country** (culture, traditions, religion)
2. **His Relatives** (Rebellion, lawbreaking)
3. **His father's house** (idols, vision, name)

Avram was being asked to *renounce his flag, renounce his relatives* and *renounce his family roots*, because they all supported his old identity and his previous way of life. **G-d was asking Avram to adopt a new identity**. The only way that Avram could become G-d's nation in the earth was by cutting himself off from the sin and iniquities in his own bloodline. *A study of how G-d planted the nation of Yisra'el within one individual* will be necessary if you want to understand how to confront generational sin and iniquity in your bloodline.

As you begin to develop your new identity in the Messiah, generational sin and iniquity will begin to emerge. *Departure from your country of origin will cause the hidden strangers to be severed from their roots.* The more you continue to develop and grow in the Messiah, the more they will starve and die.

When you decide to **act on the command** given to renounce *country, relatives and family roots,* you will encounter generational sin and iniquity in your own bloodline. The Bible tells us to become *doers* of the Word and not *hearers* only. **Doing** *activates* the power of G-d to bring about the necessary changes. Developing in the Messiah indicates **movement** in the Messiah. Generational sin and iniquity will surface when there is *a constant movement of faith* in G-d.

Avram lived *a nomadic lifestyle,* which meant, he was always on the move. Avram and his family went to Egypt because of a famine. To guard against Pharaoh's jealousy, whilst in Egypt Avram passed Sarai off as his sister. Pharaoh took Sarai into his royal household, but on discovering Avram's deception, he released her immediately and sent Avram and his family away. Whilst still **in the process** of his *faith journey,*

Avram was confronted with the lies, deception and trickery that showed up in his bloodline during a time of famine, and a time he was having to exercise great faith.[31]

b. THE ROOT

Each generation must confront their own generational sin and iniquity. You must *be aware* of the weaknesses that generational sin and iniquity have created in you, so that you can be on guard, especially when you are moving to a new territory. New territories can mean promotion in ministry, marriage or some area that requires your faith to be tested. If it's a new area, *you will be faced with a new challenge.*

Yitz'chak accepted and adopted the promise G-d made to Avraham, that he would become "a father of many." **Yitz'chak did not grow up in the country of his father's birth,** he was born and raised in the desert. He was raised in the culture of *"walking by faith."* Though Avraham gave everything he owned to Yitz'chak, Avraham recognized that he could not prevent the transference of generational sin and iniquity. So Avraham taught Yitz'chak everything he knew about the generational sin and iniquity.[32]

Avraham realized that G-d's plan to *make him into a nation* could be aborted in Yitz'chak, if he was not made aware of

---

[31] B'resheet (Genesis) 20
[32] B'resheet 25: 5

the *established weaknesses in his bloodline;* the ones Avraham knew about and the ones Yitz'chak would discover in his own journey. I believe one of the reasons why Avraham instructed Eliezer, his servant, to find Yitz'chak a wife from among his own relatives, was to help him gain a deeper understanding about the familial spirits attached to his bloodline.[33] Yitz'chak married his first cousin, Rivkah.

Not long after Yitz'chak married Rivkah (Rebekah), he found himself in an almost identical scenario to what his father Avraham experienced, prior to his birth. The circumstance was famine but the place he went to during that time, was G'rar (Gerar) and the king was Avimelekh. For fear of being killed over Rivkah's beauty, Yitz'chak told his wife to say that she was his sister. Yitz'chak's lies and deception was soon discovered.[34]

Again, in *the second generation,* Yitz'chak confronts the same generational sin and iniquity in his bloodline. He wasn't even conceived when his father Avraham told an identical lie. At that time, Yitz'chak was *a mere seed in his father's loins.* Parents seem to think that the sins they commit before they have had any children will not affect their children. However, Avraham's decision to tell Pharaoh that Sarah was his sister instead of his wife, affected Yitz'chak, even **before** he was conceived. Avraham and Sarah agreed to lie, and as

[33] B'resheet 24: 1-7
[34] B'resheet 26: 1-11

a result, their lie came to fruition in the lives of Yitz'chak and Rivkah. Many of the seeds sown in one generation, will lie dormant until identical conditions in which the seed was sown, reoccurs in the lives of relatives in the next generation.

Under the guidance of your spiritual leadership, ask the *Ruach HaKodesh* (Holy Spirit) to assist you to *expose the hidden strangers* in your bloodline. You don't need to be afraid or concerned about anything. G-d knows the end from the beginning of all our lives.[35] Explain the symptoms and what you are experiencing to someone who will stand with you in prayer. **Don't be afraid to expose the enemy and don't be ashamed** either. The hidden strangers will use *the feelings of their shame* to stop you from driving them out of your life. Shame is not of G-d.

c. THE TREE

Yitz'chak worked hard to cultivate the family tree, but he struggled to break free from the hidden strangers of His bloodline. Rivkah became pregnant with twins, during which time she noticed that *within her womb*, there was a great fight between them. She enquired of *ADONAI* about this situation:

> 23'... "There are two nations in your womb. From birth they will be two rival peoples. One of these peoples will be

---

[35] Yesha'yahu 46: 10

---

stronger than the other, and the older will serve the younger." [24] When the time for her delivery came, there were twins in her womb. [25] The first to come out was reddish and covered all over with hair, like a coat; so they named him 'Esav (Esau, "completely formed," that is, "having hair already"). [26] Then his brother emerged, with his hand holding 'Esav's heel, so he was called Ya'akov ("he catches by the heel," "he supplants").

B'resheet 25: 23-26

In the third generation, we begin to see a noticeable difference; a generational distinction taking place during Rivkah's pregnancy. The twins she carried, were **divided and at war in her womb**. This fight was revealing that something was occurring between the seed of G-d's Promise and the seed of Avraham's ancestors. The fact that Ya'akov and 'Esav were at war in their mother's womb was a revelation that the Promise G-d made to Avraham when he was just one man, was about to become *distinctive*.

d. CONCLUSION

In conclusion, Ya'akov's internal struggle revealed that G-d had called him to fight for the establishment of the promise made to his grandfather Avraham. Ya'akov was given an assignment to *aggressively fight* to close the door on generational sin and iniquity in the third and fourth generation. **By the third generation, iniquity can be annihilated, causing the fourth generation to go free.**

5 *Spending Time Alone*

L eaving the comforts of home life to spend time alone with G-d in the wilderness is the preparation that you will need to step into your purpose. The *Ruach HaKodesh* (Holy Spirit) may lead some on an assignment to another country or perhaps to spend a week away from family and friends. Others may sign up to go away on a weekend retreat where no contact with the outside world is permitted, because the specific program is to have *'a face to face encounter with G-d.'*

We all need to spend time alone in the wilderness, on a regular basis. Especially those who give their lives in the service of others. If leaders fail to do this they will most definitely experience *burnout* and those they serve will be the first to suffer. As long as you live in the *'olam hazeh*, your five physical senses will be bombarded by its data. Yes, you must continue to *fight the good fight of faith*, however **your spiritual batteries** will need to *be recharged periodically.*

If you don't **give preference to** *'your personal relationship with G-d,'* you will not be able to stand up against the enemy's assault. Spending time alone with G-d will reveal those hidden strangers within, and make you **spiritually sharp**. How can you hope to experience longevity in ministry when you are fighting an enemy within and the enemy without?

Having a personal encounter with G-d a few times a year, will keep you on track. The level of enemy attacks that you will face, depends on your specific calling. Sometimes the attacks to your personal and ministerial life are *relentless*, to the point of burnout.

At such times, it will be necessary for you to **take a sabbatical** and allow G-d to re-route your ministry, so that you will arrive at your destination, on time and intact. **Long-standing disappointments** may cause you to become wary. One of Hasatan's strategies is *the sustained attack* on the life of a worshiping believer. Hasatan's stratagem keep you focused on your pain. It is a well-known fact in the circles of leadership, that most, if not all, suffer from *long-term ministerial trauma*. Over-extending yourself is nothing short of *ministerial suicide*; a prime example of this is when the *Ruach HaKodesh* has completed His assignment and you choose to override His decision by continuing the assignment in your own strength.

Many of you feel like you have sacrificed years of your time and effort, only to be *chewed up* and *spat out*, by those in whom much of your time was invested. *You may have watched those who you considered to be faithful talmidim* (disciples), *leave without as much as a 'thank you'.* Despite all that, *you have kept on giving, only to be abused and misused.* All of these experiences are **contributing factors** to why *you feel traumatized and sick in your soul.* I want you to know that *untreated ministerial trauma* from years of service, causes a sickness of the soul that produces *bitterness*.[36] Your sickness may not be obvious to those you serve because you operate in the anointing of your calling. Sadly, **many never really see your humanity, they only see your anointing. They are there to receive and you are there to give**.

The suffering of **emotional pain,** will make you *feel drained* and cause you to become *spiritually weak*. I encourage you to *take time out* from your business schedules, in order to **reconnect with your first love**. The Father is searching for those who will worship Him in spirit and in truth. The missing formula for your life, is **G-d's Touch**. *Spending time alone in worship* with G-d is **the treatment you desperately need**.[37]

a. YESHUA SPENT REGULAR TIME ALONE

Before Yeshua began His assignment, He was driven into the wilderness by the *Ruach HaKodesh* for forty days and forty nights. He left his family home to be alone with G-d where **His sonship was tested**. *The barrenness of the wilderness, brought His flesh into subjection to HaKodesh* (the Spirit).

Physically, Yeshua experienced hunger, however, **the wilderness made Him spiritually strong**. The Bible asserts, *'Yeshua returned to the Galil in the power of the Spirit...'* Note

---

[36] Messianic Jews (Hebrews) 12: 14, 15
[37] Yochanan 4: 23, 24

that Yeshua did what His forefather Avraham did and what the children of Isra'el did when they wandered for forty years in the wilderness under Moshe's ministration.[38] This principle was established in the lives of the Patriarchs of Yisra'el, and is the prerequisite necessary to be *a sent one.*

b. YA'AKOV NEEDED TO SPEND TIME ALONE

Like his Grandfather Avraham, Ya'akov needed to spend time alone to consider his ways and the traditions of his bloodline. His assignment was to finish what his Grandfather started. **From the womb**, it was evident that Ya'akov was born with the *'Breakthrough Anointing.'* He was called to close the door on generational sin and iniquity so that Yisra'el could lay ahold of the Promise.

Generational sin and iniquity in the bloodline will *steal, kill and destroy your inheritance.* The Hidden Strangers are out to steal your inheritance by creating *weaknesses* in you. *If you are weak, you will not be able to fight.* **I believe Ya'akov was given his name from the womb, so that he would never forget that he was born to fight for the promised inheritance.** *Prior to Ya'akov's departure from his family home, he was able to secure the rights of the firstborn from his brother 'Esav, and the blessing of the firstborn son from his father,*

---

[38] Luke 4: 1-14

Yitz'chak.[39] He took his inheritance by *trickery, lies and deception.* Both Ya'akov and his mother's actions, caused a rift in their family. Another hidden stranger in Avraham and Yitz'chak's bloodline emerged when Ya'akov *usurped* his brother 'Esav and gained the advantage over him. For the first time, *the spirit of Murder* surfaced because 'Esav had planned to murder his brother Ya'akov, after his father's death. Rivkah, warned her son Ya'akov of his brother's plan and suggested that he leave home to go and live with his uncle Lavan.[40]

c. YA'AKOV WAS BORN TO BREAKTHROUGH

You've got to understand that Ya'akov was born *to break the iniquitous patterns* in his bloodline, which is why he needed to **understand his roots.** Whatever he knew was passed down to him from two generations. Both Avraham and Yitz'chak had their own struggles with the iniquitous patterns in their bloodline, however *'the Breaker Anointing'* **was given to Ya'akov.** He was purpose-built to get to grips with the hidden strangers and eject them so that *Yisra'el* could become G-d's own special possession. This is the reason why *Avraham, Yitz'chak* and *Ya'akov* are referred to as the Patriarchs of the Nation of *Yisra'el* – **they are the roots of the cultivated Olive Tree.**

---

[39] B'resheet 25: 27-34

[40] B'resheet 27: 41-44

---

d. BE KINGDOM-MINDED

G-d wants you to be fruitful and multiply, therefore, like Ya'akov, you too must become *the Freedom Fighter in your bloodline.* Too many of our leaders today, sow their time and efforts into those of their own generation, because they are not Kingdom Minded. If they were *Kingdom Minded,* they'd invest in the next generation. *G-d wants you to invest in the third and the fourth generation.* **Keep them at the forefront of your minds,** as Avraham did. He treated his son Yitz'chak, like a Nation.[41] G-d said to Avraham that He would make him into a great nation. Avraham passed this idea to his son Yitz'chak, and Yitz'chak declared the blessing of the firstborn over his son Ya'akov. Ya'akov had twelve sons and fought for the 'establishment G-d's Nation'. You see twelve is the number of *government and rule.*

e. FAMILY TRAITS

Family traits can be clearly seen, whenever family members are gathered together. You can turn such gatherings into an insightful exercise, especially when you are just beginning to learn about your family history. The older members of the family derive great pleasure from telling their younger relatives, **who** *they resemble* and **what** *character trait* the family is known by. The stories they tell usually convey the traits of the hidden strangers in the bloodline. Families tend

---

[41] B'resheet 25: 5

---

to associate a particular character trait with an individual because they are unaware that a hidden stranger even exists let alone has an influence. The elders in the families find it easy to induct each of its **new members** into the family roots because *they are innocent and vulnerable*. The elders in particular, provide the history of the ancestral lineage – the good, the bad and the ugly. **Family history provides its members with a sense of belonging and a sense of identity**.

f. THE GUARDIANS OF
YOUR ORAL HISTORY

The elders in a family are the guardians of their ancestry's oral history. *They hold the key to the historical records of the family*, including its issues, its secrets, its indiscretions, its crimes, its strengths and its weaknesses. **Some guardians**, decide, whether individually or corporately, to *deliberately withhold historical secrets for fear of being rejected*. Before the elders join their ancestors, they feel they have the responsibility to *initiate the youngest members of the family* so that they will become the *carriers of ancient ancestral traditions*. To prevent rejection, the elders may omit a few ancestral details such as: *murder, homosexuality* and *pedophilia*.

The problem is, *even if ancestral crimes are withheld, their fruits will show up in blood relations who are alive*. Whatever family you are born into, it is **the bloodline that connects you to your ancestors.** <u>You are living in the consequences of decisions made by your ancestors.</u>

Bloodlines carry the cravings and **appetites** of previous generations. Their established traditions of the past, dictates the level of relevancy they have today.

g. CONCLUSION

As you take time out of your busy life to spend time alone with G-d, I want you to know that you will never come out of the wilderness the same way you went in. *Yeshua HaMashiach* arose triumphantly from the grave to set you free from generational sin and iniquity. On His Execution Stake, Yeshua victoriously *broke through* on your behalf, so that by receiving Him you became the inheritor of the 'Breakthrough Anointing.'[42]

Ya'akov received this same 'breakthrough-anointing' from the womb. It was revealed to their mother, that the older would serve the younger. When it was Rivkah's time to give birth, 'Esav came out first, however, his twin brother Ya'akov held onto his heel. Ya'akov was called to break generational sin and iniquity in his bloodline.[43]

In Yeshua HaMashiach, *you have been given a greater anointing* to close the door on generational sin and iniquity in your bloodline.[44] I believe every leader must know and

---

[42] Colossians 3: 5-10

[43] B'resheet 25: 26-28

[44] Yesha'yahu 61: 1, 2; Luke 4: 18

understand how to liberate those assigned to their care. You must first go through the process of liberation before taking someone else through their process. A person who has been liberated can free others.

> [1] What the Messiah has freed us for is freedom! Therefore, stand firm, and don't let yourselves be tied up again to a yoke of slavery.

Galatians 5: 1

6 *Your Encounter with G-d*

As a member of the Messianic Community of Believers, it is your right to have an encounter with G-d. Yeshua paid a high price to restore your relationship with the Father. Preparing to meet with your G-d needs prayerful consideration. Every time you approach G-d, *you must dig a little deeper if you want to move a little closer.* You must ask the *Ruach HaKodesh* (Holy Spirit) to expose your sins and the sins of your forefathers. **Press in** for a deeper experience with G-d. **Always search for areas of pride in your life**, then **humble yourselves** on purpose, before the L-rd and He will lift you up.

> [8] Come close to God, and he will come close to you. Clean your hands, sinners; and purify your hearts, you double-minded people! [9] Wail, mourn, sob! Let your laughter be turned into mourning and your joy into gloom! [10] Humble yourselves before the Lord, and he will lift you up.
>
> **Ya'akov (James) 4: 8-10**

Ya'akov was moving into a closer encounter with G-d when his father Yitz'chak blessed him and commanded him not to marry any of the Hitti women. He was told to go and live with his mother's brother (his uncle) and choose a wife from one of his daughters. The job of closing the door on generational sin and iniquity in his bloodline, fell to Ya'akov a son, born in the third generation. Ya'akov spent twenty years away from home, during which time *he familiarized himself with his own family traits.* **He learned to serve and served to learn** the **ways** of his bloodline. Ya'akov was well within his rights to retaliate against his relative's bad behavior towards him. However, Ya'akov remained *humble and determined* to keep up the fight to overcome the iniquitous patterns operating within his relatives and himself. It eventually transpired that *Lavan was using his nephew, Ya'akov,* because he noticed that the favor of G-d was on his life and on everything he put his hands to.

Lavan was reluctant to let his nephew go, so for twenty years *he used trickery* to keep Ya'akov in service to him. Interestingly enough, notice how *the elder relatives* love to take ownership over the lives of the younger relatives. The struggle that began with his twin brother, in the womb of his mother, became much more intense as a shepherd working under his uncle. However, after twenty years of service, *he conquered the five territories of relationship.* Ya'akov encountered hidden strangers in the territories of the following areas:

Table 5: **Confronted the Hidden Strangers in five Territories of the Bloodline**

1.	**Lavan**	*Iniquitous patterns in the bloodline, family traits,*
2.	**Shepherd**	*Lavan's wealth increased by association*
3.	**Father**	*Establishing the correct example for posterity*
4.	**Husband**	*Good husband and provider*
5.	**Servant**	*Understood accountability to leadership*

a. YA'AKOV RETURNS TO THE WOMB

Ya'akov's mission in life was the establishment of G-d's rule on earth. His was called from the womb *to overturn the opposition in his bloodline*. These days we commonly use the term '**blood**' when referring to a sibling. The same term is used to make the distinction between the two bloodlines who were at war within Rivkah's womb. In fact, the Bible refers to these two bloodlines as '*two nations*.'[45] I believe that *the spiritual warfare going on within Rivkah's womb was a fight for supremacy*; the hidden stranger was already at war with the Seed of the Promise. Rivkah **felt the war** but **she couldn't see the war**.

A fight for G-d's Nation began in the womb between to two blood brothers. 'Esav was ungodly and *showed little value for his birthright*. Ya'akov valued 'Esav's birthright, because he carried the DNA of the promise made to Avraham. The value of Ya'akov's name is seven, and seven means maturity or completion. Ya'akov kept his focus on the Promise, in order to bring each of his assignments to completion. *The concept of seven* is repeated throughout the life of Ya'akov.

Ya'akov's assigned purpose was two-fold: Firstly, he was called to **close the door** on generational sin and iniquity in his bloodline, and secondly, he was called to **open the door** of G-d's Kingdom rule in his bloodline. G-d's Kingdom rule

---

[45] B'resheet 25: 22, 23

was established in the Twelve Tribes of Yisra'el. If you have been called by G-d to birth a great ministry in the earth, **don't expect your life to be easy.** *You will have to complete multiple assignments in order to establish the foundation.* Yet it is **the foundation of your ministry that will support you on your** *mountaintops* **and in your** *valleys.* Ya'akov's journey tells us that building the foundation starts with a personal reordering before we are ready to reorder the lives of others.

An encounter with G-d begins with your bloodline. **Whenever G-d looks at you, He sees you in your blood.**[46] *He knows* **who** *the lawbreakers are,* **what** *laws were broken,* **when** *they were broken,* **where** *to find them and* **how** *they affect your life today.* If G-d identifies you in your blood, you must identify yourself in relation to your bloodline. *One of the Adversary's strategies in a believer's life is to* **prevent** *them from knowing anything about their bloodline.* The Adversary knows that the hidden workers of iniquity will have no place to hide, the day you find out **who** they are and **where** they are hiding in your bloodline.

After twenty years of waging war in his bloodline, Ya'akov realized that he had to conclude the cycle. *His fight began with 'Esav and concluded with 'Esav, in order to close that chapter.* 'Esav didn't understand why he wanted his brother dead, but Ya'akov did understand, which is why *fear enveloped him as he approached* 'Esav. *It is difficult to separate yourself from the*

---

[46] Yechezk'el 16:6

tradition and culture of your family. Whenever members of a family unite, the hidden strangers in the bloodline *have a stronger influence.* This is why Ya'akov's encounter with G-d was the intervention he needed, in order to confront the spirit of Fear. The night before Ya'akov was due to meet his brother, for the first time after twenty years, the *Torah* says, *'... Ya'akov was left alone. Then some man wrestled with him until daybreak.'* For Ya'akov, wrestling with a man all night, represented *the culmination of a twenty-year battle.* **The one thing that seemed to have alluded Ya'akov was the truth of who he was.** Ya'akov wrestled all night until he received a breakthrough that was complete; a breakthrough that completed the blessing given to his grandfather Avraham.

b. BATTLE AT THE GATES

Ya'akov wrestled with the Man for *the final part of his blessing* until daybreak. You have to understand that his struggle was no ordinary struggle. *Ya'akov was engaged in a battle to exchange a curse for a blessing in his bloodline.* Ya'akov's bloody warfare finally put an end to the reign of the hidden strangers in his bloodline. **All** the Strongmen came to the frontlines in full force; *they battled for their existence* in the lives of Ya'akov's family.

Ya'akov was able to **see** and **recognize** exactly **who** the strangers of his bloodline were. **He saw their reflection in the Face of G-d.** The breaking of the dawn signaled Ya'akov's own breakthrough because it was at that point, a single question was asked, *"What is your name?"* And in shock of realization, Ya'akov whispered, *"**supplanter**, **schemer**, **trickster**, and **swindler**."* These four evil strongmen represented the roots behind the curse that threatened to overthrow G-d's Promise to Avraham, Yitz'chak and Ya'akov.

c. NAME CHANGE, DNA CHANGE

I firmly believe that the name *Yisra'el*, represents the DNA change that occurred in the bloodline of Avraham, Yitz'chak Ya'akov and the Twelve sons of Yisra'el. **The change of name was also a change of status.** *Ya'akov's new birth, elevated him from the second son, to take his rightful position amongst the Nations, as G-d's firstborn son.* Before Ya'akov finally came face to face with his brother 'Esav, *he recognized that a permanent separation had occurred in his bloodline. Esav and Ya'akov were two different nations.*[47] Today, DNA Testing can reveal whether a person is of the Hebraic bloodline and specifically whether they carry the DNA Marker of a *cohen*. Imagine, G-d's Promise changed the DNA of *a three-generational bloodline* that originated in Iraq!

> 23 You have been regenerated (born again), not from a mortal origin (seed, **sperm**), but from the one that is immortal by the *ever* living and lasting **Word of God**.
>
> **1Peter 1: 23 AMP**

---

[47] B'resheet 33: 1-17

Ya'akov's life-long struggle to be free prepared him to face the trauma he suffered in the womb and the perpetrator of that trauma. After having *a face-to-face encounter with G-d*, Ya'akov was prepared to confront *his greatest Fear*. 'Esav represented Ya'akov's greatest fear, even though he was liberated from the spirit of Fear the day before. Though *the feeling* of fear was still a reality for Ya'akov, **by faith**, he was prepared to approach the brother who had planned to murder him, some twenty years earlier.

d. CONCLUSION

A true encounter with G-d will close the door on generational sin and iniquity that has been plaguing your life. However, to be free, you must make a firm decision to fight to be free from the hidden strangers in your bloodline.[48] *Keep holding your ground until you get a 'breakthrough.'*[49] *Keep pressing forward to have a face-to-face encounter with G-d.* **Remember, Ya'akov wrestled with G-d in order to see His face, because in G-d's face he saw a reflection of himself.**[50] G-d is Light, and His presence will expose your sin and iniquity. When you have successfully conquered the enemy's strongholds in your life, you will be ready to work in **a greater level of partnership with G-d.**

---

[48] B'resheet 32: 25
[49] B'resheet 32: 26
[50] B'resheet 32: 27

7 Your Encounter with Yeshua

The only person that can prepare you to meet G-d is Yeshua. An encounter with Yeshua, will completely transform your life and bring you back into G-d's perfect plan. In order to experience this life-changing transformation, you must be *updated* by G-d's Word. G-d's Word needs to be applied to your life like bandages to a wound. David recognized that he was a sinner from the moment his mother conceived him. He was born guilty.[51] I want you to know that sin inflicts deep wounds in your soul, which can manifest in a range of physical and mental illnesses. To survive in our world, we have built up *a wall of resistance to polemic assault*. Negative words, cause deep wounds that aren't visible to the naked eye. Physicians can prescribe medicines that will treat your symptoms temporarily, however, G-d is able to heal *the cause* of your sicknesses permanently. Hallelujah!

> [6] From the sole of the foot to the head **there is nothing healthy**, only wounds, bruises and festering sores that haven't been dressed or bandaged or softened up with oil.
>
> **Yesha'yahu (Isaiah) 1: 6**

---

[51] Tehillim (Psalm) 51: 5

a. PREPARE TO MEET YOUR G-D

Some of you became members of the Messianic Community of Believers recently, and there are those of you who are seasoned believers. Whether you are a new believer or a leader of a congregation, you were being prepared to have an encounter with G-d from the time you were conceived in your mother's womb. Your parents may have said you were a mistake, however, in G-d's eyes **you are certainly not a mistake.** <u>G-d made a plan for you, in His love.</u>[52] David, in a moment of intimacy, expressed his heart in a song he wrote:

> [13] For you fashioned my innermost being, you knit me together in my mother's womb. [14] I thank you because I am awesomely made, wonderfully; your works are wonders – I know this very well. [15] My bones were not hidden from you when I was being made in secret, intricately woven in the depths of the earth. [16] **Your eyes could see me as an embryo**, but in your book all my days were already written; my days had been shaped before any of them existed.
>
> **Tehillim (Psalm) 139: 13-16**

G-d turns all your life experiences into lessons. G-d will use your country, your people group and your family, to train you. *We can all testify to having had a past life, without G-d in it. We can testify to having no real understanding about the **thirst** for an intimate relationship with our Creator.* At one time, **your thirst**, caused you to lose direction, it moved you away from

---

[52] Ephesians 1: 4

G-d's original purpose for your life. Only an encounter with Yeshua can get you back on the right track. **Accepting** Yeshua as *ADONAI* will point you in the right direction. **Knowing** Yeshua prepares you to meet the Father.

> [6] Yeshua said, "I AM the Way – and the Truth and the Life; no one comes to the Father except through me. [7] Because you have known me, you will also know my Father; from now on, you do know him – in fact, you have seen him."
>
> **Yochanan (John) 14: 6, 7**

Remember, when Ya'akov looked into the face of the Man, (*Whom I believed to have been the pre-incarnate Son of G-d*), he was shocked at what he saw. *For the first time, Ya'akov came face to face with his **true** reflection.* He was able to identify, acknowledge and take responsibility for the nefarious works of the Hidden Strangers in his bloodline.[53] The three Patriarchs were each given an assignment to establish G-d's Nation in the earth. However, *the responsibility for closing the door on generational sin and iniquity fell to Ya'akov.* It was a job that Ya'akov was equipped to do and he fought to complete each step.

*You're calling is accompanied by the anointing to bring your assignments to completion, despite the obstacles. G-d will never give you more than you can handle and **His plan for your life can only be aborted if you decide to give up.***

---

[53] Genesis 32: 24-28 AMP

b. YOUR ILLICIT LOVE AFFAIR
WITH THE WORLD

You need to be aware that *your encounter with the world has had a detrimental effect on your life*. On a daily basis, this world has been feeding your mind, will and emotions, on a diet of lies and deception; leaving you feeling frustrated. As a result, **you have developed an insatiable appetite for things that will bring you to rack and ruin**.

You pursued a pathway that this world offered, and searched for happiness and contentment in all the wrong places. *Friendship with this world has caused you to covet what others have and when you don't get what you want, your unfulfilled desires produce a mindset that harbors murderous intentions.* You can't be happy for someone else's success because you burn with envy. Your pursuit of **fame, money** and **pleasure**, has made you an enemy of G-d.

> [4] You [are like] unfaithful wives [having illicit love affairs with the world and breaking your marriage vows to God]! Do you not know that being the world's friend is being God's enemy? So whoever chooses to be a friend of the world takes his stand as an enemy of God.
>
> **James 4: 4 AMP**

c. FAME

We are living in the days where it isn't inconceivable to achieve fame. Fame is one of the biggest illusions in our world today. Those who possess a rare gift can go viral in a hot minute and this world has gone ballistic in providing platforms to showcase these gifted individuals. Platforms such as, **Britain's Got Talent, American Idol** and **X Factor** have reproduced copies or versions worldwide. The devil is working hard to feed *the desire for fame* and *celebrity status.* Our world has redefined fame and stardom as achieving ultimate happiness, contentment and even world domination. The following list covers the most coveted jobs:

- Singer/Songwriter (solo artistes, rappers, R&B, classical, contemporary, jazz, blues)
- Actors & Actresses (film/theatre)
- Record Producers (sound engineers)
- Film Producer/Director
- TV Camera Operators
- Musicians
- Radio Broadcasters
- Radio Presenters
- Radio Actors
- Contemporary Dancers
- Ballet Dancers
- Disc Jockey (DJ's)
- TV Presenters
- News Broadcasters

d. MONEY

Money is one of the greatest addictions in our world. You can secure a high status in this life if you have a lot of money. *The god of this world has turned money into its greatest commodity.* '**Work for the money**' is a song that the whole world sings. Members of the elite, the rich and famous have *sold their souls to the devil* for money.[54] Their actions have created a deliberate division between '*the haves*' and '*the have nots.*' The elites of this world have been placed in positions of great power and control over the underprivileged. However, **the great deception** *is that both the privileged and the underprivileged are slaves in the devil's game.* G-d deserves to be the center of our love, <u>instead of money</u>. Money is a blessing when it is working for the good and when it is a blessing to others. Money becomes a curse when it is treated like treasure that is stored in the heart.

> [19] Do not gather and heap up and store up for yourselves treasures on earth, where moth and rust and worm consume and destroy, and where thieves break through and steal. [20] But gather and heap up and store for yourselves treasures in heaven, where neither moth nor rust nor worm consume and destroy, and where thieves do not break through and steal; [21] For **where you treasure is, there will your heart** be also.

Matthew 6: 19-21 AMP

e. PLEASURE

The search for pleasure is a symptom of an underlying thirst that, out of balance, has destroyed homes and ruined marriages. *Our world today, has a preoccupation with sexual pleasure.* It is common for married couples to have

---

[54] 1 Timothy 6: 10

extramarital relationships. Many men pay for the services of a prostitute, others frequently indulge in pornography.

If you don't have an intimate relationship with G-d, you will search for pleasure from this world. Unhappiness is the result of having a relationship with the world. *The world programmed you to have a thirst that it can never quench.* If you are reading this book, you have entered a new season; a season where you will search for true happiness and find it. True happiness is *Yeshua HaMashiach*.

f. YESHUA CAN PINPOINT THE CAUSE OF YOUR THIRST

Yeshua can identify *the thirst common to all those who have not experienced the New Birth*. On His way to Galil (Galilee), it was necessary for Him to pass through Shomron (Samaria). Yeshua's purpose in Shomron was to have **a face-to-face encounter with a woman who had a thirst**.

> [5] He came to a town in Shomron called Sh'khem, near the field Ya'akov had given to his son Yosef. [6] Ya'akov's Well was there; so Yeshua, exhausted from his travel, sat down by the well; it was about noon. [7] A woman from Shomron came to draw some water; and Yeshua said to her, "Give me a drink of water." [8] (His *talmidim* had gone into town to buy food.) [9] The woman from Shomron said to him, "How is it that you, a Jew, ask for water from me, a woman of Shomron?" (For Jews don't associate with people from Shomron.) [10] Yeshua answered her, "If you knew God's gift, that is, who it is saying to you, 'Give me a drink of water,'

then you would have asked him; and he would have given you living water."

Yochanan 4: 5 – 10

Yeshua had a specific assignment to fulfill in Shomron. Ya'akov's Well was the location of his assignment and *the woman's thirst* was the problem that needed His attention. Exhausted and thirsty from his travel, Yeshua sat down at Ya'akov's Well. Now remember it was Ya'akov who was given the responsibility to close the door on the three-generational sin and iniquity in his bloodline. Ya'akov identified the Hidden Strangers and their iniquitous patterns in his relatives. He acknowledged that He represented them; living and dead, because he carried their iniquities in his own blood.

Yeshua sat by the Well that belonged to *His forefather* because he was getting ready to deal with the generational sins and iniquities of a whole town *through one woman*. **She was the key** that could bring her town into total liberation, or keep them in bondage. Yeshua introduces Himself to a woman whose life was an open book before His eyes. His first words were not a greeting, such as '*Hello.*'

Yeshua pinpointed her thirst by asking her to give Him a drink. A face-to-face encounter with Yeshua will not be based on 'small talk,' *it will pinpoint the cause*. Yeshua knew that the woman had a particular **thirst that only He could quench**, and that *her particular thirst caused her to commit* *shameful acts that made her feel cheap and degraded.* The woman began to highlight the fact that antagonism still exists between the Jews and people from Shomron (the Samaritans). She wanted to know why He would be asking her for a drink. Yeshua pointed out to the woman that He was indeed G-d's gift of *mayim chayim* (living water) sent to quench her particular thirst. All that was required of her, was to **simply ask.**[55]

> [11] She said to him, "Sir, you don't have a bucket, and the well is deep; so where do you get this 'living water'? [12] You aren't greater than our father Ya'akov, are you? He gave us this well and drank from it, and so did his sons and his cattle." [13] Yeshua answered, "Everyone who drinks this water will get thirsty again, [14] but **whoever drinks the water I will give him will never be thirsty again!** On the contrary, the water I give him will become a spring of water inside him, welling up into eternal life!"

> **Yochanan 4: 11 - 14**

Until you have a face-to-face encounter with Yeshua, you will never be able to satisfy the craving or quench the thirst of a three-generational bloodline. An encounter with the world will have you caught in *a cycle of gorging yourself* until you become addicted. In fact, the god of this world offers ***addictive solutions*** as his alternative to ***true satisfaction,*** *which is a state of being that comes only from G-d.*

---

[55] Mattityahu 7:7

---

15 "**Sir, give me this water**," the woman said to him, "so that I won't have to be thirsty and keep coming here to draw water." 16 He said to her, "Go, call your husband, and come back." 17 She answered, "I don't have a husband." Yeshua said to her, "You're right, you don't have a husband! 18 You've had five husbands in the past, and you're not married to the man you're living with now! You've spoken the truth!"

Yochanan 4: 15 – 18

The woman makes the same mistake we all make, in thinking that we can satisfy a spiritual thirst in a natural way. We tend to try and fix a problem that only G-d can fix, and then after years of looking in many different places, Boom! we have one encounter with Yeshua that changes everything.

For years prior to her encounter with Yeshua, the woman from Shomron (Samaria), had a colourful past where she fell into relationships with many men. *A confrontation with **the Words** of Yeshua*, reveals her whole life. The woman from Shomron could not deny that **the Word revealed** aspects of her life that she would rather have kept hidden. *The woman became **convicted** about her wrong choices and **honest** about her sins.*

As soon as the woman said, *"Sir, give me this water so that I won't have to be thirsty and keep coming here to draw water,"* **Yeshua put His finger on <u>the cause</u> of her thirst** when He said, *"Go, call your husband, and come back."* When the woman answered, *"I don't have a husband,"* Yeshua went on to reveal that the woman had five husbands in the past and the man with whom she currently resided, is not her husband. In her search to find satisfaction in the multiple male friends she dated, the woman of Shomron *formed an addiction to men.* No matter how much she yearned for them, *they could never quench her thirst.* Yeshua showed the woman that she had **five Adams**, and the only **Adam** that was able to quench her thirst, was standing in front of her.

g. EMOTIONAL RESTORATION

The woman of Shomron experienced emotional restoration after her encounter with Yeshua. He removed *the emptiness, anxiety, unhappiness* and *embarrassment* from her life, and *gave her a new heart and a new start.* Yeshua made the woman of Shomron into **a vessel of honor** and *realigned her emotions.* She left the encounter with Yeshua, *a transformed individual,* because she perceived the importance of this meeting as *an encounter that was supernatural.* All the townsmen who knew her and the life she had led in the past, were impacted by her testimony. They could also **see** the transformation in her. As a result of *her transformation* and *her testimony,* many people from her town came to faith in Yeshua.[56] The woman of Shomron became a great missionary and possibly the first female Evangelist in the *B'rit Hadashah* (New Testament).

---

[56] Yochanan 4: 39

---

h. SPIRITUAL RESTORATION

A physical problem always has a spiritual root. *Yeshua HaMashiach* will always pinpoint the primary cause of your problem. You may not hear his audible voice, however, the number one way in which He will communicate with you, is through His Word. *G-d speaks, every time you sit under the anointed teaching or the preaching of His Word.* When you begin to realize that the light of *the Word is searching your innermost parts*, looking to home-in on a particular area of darkness, *you will know that your life is under the scrutiny of G-d's eye.*[57]

When *you start to get uncomfortable* under G-d's spotlight, this is a sign that the anointing of the Prophet is in operation.[58] *Your continued submission* to the Word that is exposing a hidden stranger in your bloodline, shows that you are willing to **bow down** to ADONAI.

> [12] See, the Word of God is alive! It is at work and is sharper than any double-edged sword – it cuts right through to where soul meets spirit and joint meets marrow, and it is quick to judge the inner reflections and attitudes of the heart.
>
> **Messianic Jews** (Hebrews) **4: 12**

---

[57] Mishlei (Proverbs) 20: 27
[58] Yochanan 4: 19

The Woman of Shomron had been suppressing a need to worship. For many years, her thirst for the attentions of men had masked her need to worship. We sometimes make a man or a woman *the object of our worship,* however we soon find out, that neither one of them are able satisfy our needs. We were created to worship G-d alone and if we're not doing this, we will try to satisfy our *need to worship* by having *multiple partners.* **If people or things become the object of our worship, will there be any room left to worship G-d?** When a spiritual correction has taken place within, you will begin to see that *true worship* doesn't take place in a worship service, synagogue or church building. True Worship is the attitude of your heart towards G-d.[59]

i. YOUR TRANSFORMATION

What happens during your encounter with Yeshua, to a large extent, **depends on your cooperation with Him.** The measure of how much you know the L-rd, will give Him the opportunity to totally transform your life. The question is: *'How deep are you prepared to let the healing Word of G-d penetrate your life?'* In order to experience a life-changing transformation, you will, more than likely, need to **go out of town** where friends and family cannot reach you. *Anything and everything that will hinder you from experiencing a deeper relationship with G-d, must be removed.* Getting **away from all external distractions** will help you to *become empty.*

---

[59] Yochanan 4: 20-24

The next thing that is of utmost importance to the process of your transformation is to **stay open**. This means to lay aside your preconceived ideas and allow the anointed Word to challenge you. If you have decided to shut down, you are resisting and will not be open. If you are experiencing *feelings of resistance*, it is because **the hidden strangers are threatened**. When you have had an encounter with Yeshua, He will bring your past history to an end and usher you into a new spiritual era and a new beginning.

The Woman of Shomron was an adulterer who had lost the respect of her people. *Yeshua was already at Ya'akov's Well waiting to address her thirst* because she was at *the critical point* for change. She'd had enough of trying to solve the problem she had with men. **They all offered the same solution but were not able to make good on their promises**. An encounter with Yeshua however, opened her eyes to see exactly where the problem was located.

j. CONCLUSION

Your search for respect and credibility, in a man or a woman, in your place of work, or in your society, has led you to the only person who is able to break generational sin and iniquity in your bloodline. His name is Yeshua HaMashiach. Hallelujah! **Your transformation will give you a testimony revealing the Gospel of Salvation as being more than a New Birth experience**. You will be able to testify about being free from particular iniquitous patterns where there

<u>are **noticeable changes** that cause many people to be brought to faith in the Messiah</u>. In other words, an encounter with Yeshua will impact your ministry with signs, wonders and miracles following.

> [29] Come, see a man who told me everything I've ever done. Could it be that this is the Messiah? [30] They left the town and began coming toward him.
>
> **Yochanan 4: 29, 30**

8 Teraphim, Family Idols

The Teraphim are small images or cult objects used as domestic deities or oracles used by ancient Semitic peoples. They are believed to be, givers of prosperity and were, in many instances, modelled to preserve the resemblance of an ancestor. The Teraphim are *household gods* or *family idols* whose central stronghold in a family, is the bloodline. Each new member is initiated and dedicated to serve this Familial spirit. *ADONAI* said to Avram, *"Get yourself out of your country, away from your kinsmen and away from your father's house..."*[60] Avram was commanded to separate himself from his father's house. This separation did not mean that Avram no longer loved his family, it meant he was commanded to renounce all idols associated with his family.

Family idols are carved images made to resemble influential ancestors, or they can be carved images of animals. These images are the gods that many families turn to for health, wealth, prosperity and long life. *It is not unusual for family members to carry a miniature version of their god on a bracelet or on a necklace; like a Good Luck charm.* Both charms and household idols are **entry points** for the generational curses and iniquitous patterns to take root in your lives.

---

[60] B'resheet 12: 1

It is *the spirit attached to these charms and household idols* that is set apart for destruction. Why? Any object that is idolized, by a person, a family or a nation, has a spirit assigned to that object. The Devil gets the worship that is directed at any idol. **If the idol is deemed as cursed by** ADONAI **your G-d, it is because the spirit behind it is cursed.** If you worship idols or charms you will also share in the curse that is on them. **If the idol is installed in your house, members of your household will also share in the curse that is on the idol, whether knowingly or unknowingly.**

> [25] You are to burn up completely the carved statues of their gods. Don't be greedy for the silver or the gold on them; don't take it with you, or you will be trapped by it; for it is abhorrent to ADONAI your God. [26] Don't bring something abhorrent into your house, or **you will share in the curse that is on it;** instead, you are to detest it completely, loathe it utterly; for it is set apart for destruction.
>
> D'varim 7: 25-26

The Teraphim is also known as the *Family Physician* because its influence works best on the members it owns. Our identification with family, relies primarily on the system of belief established within our own ancestral line. **Systems of belief are handed down through family traditions and are commonly known, *'old wives tales'* or *'old sayings.'*** Ancient sayings and *old time stories* keep familial spirits alive in the memories of the current generation.

A closely-knit family will close ranks, as a generally rule, in order to preserve their system of belief. The elders use images such as *photographs, paintings* and *stories* to **preserve the Familial spirit** attached to the bloodline. Certain character traits related to the family idol can be identified as the prominent feature of a family group. The teraphim can be *identified through the habits* of the bloodline to which they are assigned. For instance, some families display distinct characteristics, such as **pride and loftiness** whilst other families may struggle with **mental weaknesses**.

The **most prominent** family traits identified, have the **deepest roots.** This is the reason why, the eldest living relatives in a family tend to be the carriers of their generational roots, particularly **those who have a sense of family pride**. The wisdom attached to the elders make them the obvious **carriers** and **maintainers** of the family's idols.

A Familial spirit will express *a craving to exist and to breathe within the bloodline in which they are* assigned. Whenever a decision is to be made, **the demonic influence** will find ways to *pervert the truth*, in order to annihilate any sign of G-d's DNA. They are assigned to ensure that lawlessness reigns in the current generation. The Familial spirit's commitment is to stand up against any threat to compromise the craving they have, to destroy righteousness toward G-d within their human family. Their primary aim is to STEAL, KILL and DESTROY.

In order to reinforce lawlessness within the bloodline, *parents teach their children how to keep the traditions of their forefathers.* **Whenever members of a bloodline become parents, a hidden stranger; that is, a spiritual parent will also be assigned.** The hidden work of the spiritual parents is to strongly influence the decisions making process of their physical counterparts. Familial spirits will cause lawlessness to flourish in the lives of each new member. This is the purpose of their existence.

One of the ways in which children are taught to submit to the hidden stranger in their family, is when parents install a teraphim in their home. Family idols come in many different shapes and sizes. The more common idols are the, *carved wooden masks, statues of human beings, animals, birds, sea creatures* and images that are captured in *photographs.*

a. THE LIVING ROOM

Parents, knowingly or unknowingly, **turn their living rooms into altars of worship**. Apart from the furnishing, a living room is usually decorated with all kinds of images; some historical and others may be recent installations. **If an image of any kind, receives worship, it is believed to have some kind of power**. <u>If you grew up in a family of idol worshippers, and was taught to worship those idols, you were being trained to submit to the familial spirit attached to your bloodline.</u> The question here is; *who or what where you taught to focus on during your times of meditation? Did you set* *your affections on the Creator or on the things He created?*[61] In many homes, *household images are accepted as a crucial part of a family's spiritual development.* Family idols can give its members *a false sense of peace* and feelings of tranquillity, which is why they are accepted as **household physicians**.

I stayed in the home of an artist friend for a short period of time. On her living room walls I noticed a carved bull's head, paintings of men dressed as ballerinas and other paintings that offended my spirit. Her mantelpiece and side table boasted a display of Buddhist idols; some were busts and others were miniature images that looked human. On the floor, I noticed a *three-foot high* image of a man that looked like it was made from ivory. I was certain this image represented the Devil because it had a long tail and two blunt horns which looked like they were cut short; a bit like the movie character called *Hell boy.*

Though I was encouraged to make myself at home in her living room, I couldn't bring myself to sit amongst her idols. My *spiritual senses* were immediately *on red alert* because I knew that those images, paintings and sculptures *attracted evil spirits* to share the home of the artist who owned them. She didn't realize that they took ownership of her life. After a while, this artist friend of mine asked why I never sat in her living room. She said that many of her friends found that room to be *quite a peaceful space.* Hesitantly, I told her that I

---

[61] D'varim (Deuteronomy) 5: 8 - 10

didn't feel comfortable in her living room and that I was fine to relax in my room upstairs. Well, my friend didn't stop asking me why I felt uncomfortable relaxing in her living room, until I told her that I wasn't happy with some of her paintings, images and sculptures. I thought she'd be happy with the answer I gave and discontinue the questioning, because the last thing I wanted to do was criticize anything she held in high regard.

Furthermore, I could sense the *defence* behind her query; *the hidden stranger* was looking to shut me up. In her usual polite voice, she asked if I could point out which images were offensive to me. I pointed out only a few, just because, as a guest, I didn't want to offend her in her own home. However, she continued to ask if there was anything else that offended me. Finally, I mentioned the *three-foot tall* image that was partially hidden behind a stack of her paintings on the floor. I looked her in the eye from across the kitchen and said, *'I had noticed that horrible sculpture partially hidden behind some of your painting that, in my opinion, represents the Devil. That sculpture is evil and has a spirit of Death attached to it.'*

My friend nodded her head in agreement and said, *'Yes, you're right. That sculpture is Death'* I nodded my head in agreement and said, *'Yes, I know.'* She went on to unfold the sad story behind the sculpture. The sculpture of the Devil was given to my friend as a present, by a sculptor who she knew. The woman who made the sculpture committed suicide and her partner committed suicide not too long after her. Though her expression was somewhat muted, I sensed her surprize at my spiritual accuracy. She immediately went into her living room, wrapped that evil sculpture in bubble wrap and took it out of the house. I doubt if she will ever put that evil sculpture back in her home.

Families form attachments to their idols; they occupy a prime position in their homes and in their hearts. We have many images that have *sentimental value* to us because they belonged to a relative who has passed on. Be careful about keeping idols which hold sentimental value, especially those given by the elders in your family; they may be access points for generational curses. Ask the Ruach HaKodesh (Holy Spirit) to give you clarity concerning the pictures, sculptures, jewellery, statutes and charms that you have inherited.

b. IMAGING

Focusing on, paying attention to or *spending time with,* are phrases that express an act of worship. These three phrases show us that **the object of worship** and **the worshiper** are both engaged in the act of worship. **The act of worship leaves a deep impression in the soul, in fact, idol worship will enable the worshiper to capture the image of the idol and store it in the memory.** Idol worshipers can offer worship to their gods whilst on the move, simply by *using their imagination to recreate* their idols.

c. HOUSEHOLD IMAGES

Household images are stored in two places of prominence:

1. **The Family Home** – *the most prominent place in the house*.
2. **The Soul** – *the mind, will and emotions*.

Because G-d wired the human Soul to feed, we are able to *capture data* through our five senses and store them in the memory bank of our mind, will and emotions. **Images stored in the human Soul are like treasured bits of information locked in a safe.**

d. RE-CALL, RE-MEMBER AND IMITATE

To conduct your lives, you use the information collected and stored in your memory banks. Anything you *do* or *say*, is first retrieved from your memory bank, where you are able to **recall them, re-member them** and **imitate them**. Reassembling an image, occurs in the human Soul. After assembling the images that were stored in your memory bank, you will be able to reproduce copies through your *'words'* and *'actions'*.

Your external environment is mirrored in your Soul, which is why G-d's Word tells us that we should not be conformed to the standards of the *'olam hazeh* (this world). If you continue to set your affections on the things of this world, you are bound to produce 'words' and 'actions' that come from this world.[62]

> [3] For although we do live in the world, we do not wage war in a worldly way; [4] because the weapons we use to wage war are not worldly. On the contrary, they have God's power for demolishing strongholds. We demolish arguments. [5] any every arrogance that raises itself up against the knowledge of God; **we take every thought captive and <u>make it</u> obey the Messiah.** [6] And when you have become completely obedient, then we will be ready to punish every act of disobedience.
>
> **2 Corinthians 10: 3 – 6**

Because Familial spirits produce their traits in us, when G-d looks into our bloodline, He sees us as *partakers* of the curse that is reserved for them. Why? Because we bring them to life by **'an act of our own will.'**[63]

e. CONCLUSION

G-d will test the thing that you have invested the most time in. He will place you on His scales to see whether your worship of Him is found *wanting*. We cannot be pleasing to G-d or fulfil His purpose for our lives, if we are disconnected from Him. If you feel like you are disconnected from G-d, check the area of your worship to see whether He is getting

---

[62] Romans 12: 1, 2

[63] Shof'tim (Judges) 2: 10 - 15

His due adoration from you. Some of the signs that reveal *a disconnect* from G-d are: *the inability to hear His voice, feeling spiritually sluggish, listening to the world instead of listening to G-d's Word,* or *slipping back into old habits from which you were delivered.* <u>If you feel like there is a huge gulf between you and G-d, I encourage you to get back into right standing with Him immediately</u>. The quickest way to get rid of guilt is to **acknowledge, confess** and **repent** of your sins. G-d is trustworthy and just, he will forgive you and purify you from all wrongdoing.[64] Make a decision to include repentance in your lifestyle of worship – you won't regret it!

> [1] How blessed are those whose offense is forgiven, those whose sin is covered! [2] How blessed those to whom *ADONAI* imputes no guilt, in whose spirit is no deceit!
> [3] **When I kept silent**, my bones wasted away because of my groaning all day long; [4] day and night your hand was heavy on me; the sap in me dried up as in a summer drought. [5] When I acknowledged my sin to you, **when I stopped concealing my guilt**, and said, "**I will confess my offenses to *ADONAI***"; then you, you forgave the guilt of my sin. [6] This is what everyone faithful should pray at a time when you can be found. Then, when the floodwaters are raging, they will not reach to him. [7] You are a hiding-place for me, you will keep me from distress; you will surround me with songs of deliverance.
>
> **Tehillim 32: 1 - 7**

---

[64] 1 Yochanan 1: 9

9 *Breaking Down Satanic Altars*

Demonic portals are located in every place where there is a satanic altar. Satanic worship creates an access point that allows demonic spirits to engage with live worshippers. Families tend to allocate a special place in their Living Rooms where their idols can receive worship. Whether in a home or on top of a hill, altars are given *a place of prominence* that is central to worship. A worshipper must *climb towards a culmination,* in order to attain complete spiritual engagement.

a. DRUG HOUSE

A Drug House is a residential home where mind-altering drugs are available for sale to anyone who wishes to purchase them. It is also the place where drugs are packaged and sent out by young boys and girls called, 'runners.' A place that permits the use of drugs is in effect, a satanic altar.

The job of a runner is to target the underprivileged and vulnerable, who live on rundown Estates, go to the worse Schools and individuals who are rejected by their own families. Drug Houses are like *witch covens*; an operation that is established upon a network of lies. The drug dealers are *modern day mediums* who weave a network of deception, in order to draw their victims into a false sense of security. The influence of their mind-altering drugs, leaves their clients in *a state of suspension* and **wide-open to demonic possession**. These modern-day mediums are *agents of Hasatan* and are *influenced by familiar spirits*, who have both the rich and the poor at their mercy. Here is what the *Torah* has to say about familiar spirits: "Do not turn to *spirit-mediums* or *sorcerers*; don't seek them out, to be defiled by them; I am **ADONAI** your G-d."[65] Drug dealers are mediums who have familiar spirits assigned to them; they are wizards. G-d tells us **that if we seek to engage with them, we will become defiled**.

b. THE SPIRIT OF BONDAGE

The **spirit of Fear** is usually assisted by the **spirit of Bondage**. They are jointly assigned to demobilize the human mind, in order to take control of *the powers* of the mind, will and emotions. Any kind of addiction is a manifestation of the spirit of Bondage and indicates that the individual does **not have full control** of the faculties in the Self-life.

c. APPETITES AND CRAVINGS

Evil spirits have a *craving* to **share** your life and a *thirst* that is out of control. The god of this world has set up a system that will cater for the appetites of *hidden strangers*; knowing full well that they can never be satisfied. Hidden strangers are *not licensed* to live your life, which is why they remain

---

[65] Vayikra (Leviticus) 19: 31

hidden in the darkened places in the mind. Demons, evil spirits or hidden strangers are licensed to dwell in the darkness whether you are conscious of their presence or not. They will use lies, trickery and deceit to remain undetected in your life.

d. HIDDEN STRANGERS REVEALED

Unclean spirits, demons or evil spirits don't just walk into your life; **they enter by an invitation given or by an opportunity taken**. Whenever you break G-d's law, you give demons the opportunity to enter your life whether knowingly or unknowingly. You break G-d's law whenever you commit a sin and if you continue in that sin, you will eventually be controlled by an evil spirit.

In many ways, the sins that believers or nonbelievers commit during their lifetime, are indirectly influenced by the sins of their forefathers. The sins of our forefathers are called **iniquities** because *they are no longer living*. We have inherited the sins they committed because we are related to them. **Iniquities** are the sins committed by your ancestors; they are the hidden strangers in your bloodline. It is therefore imperative to conduct a detailed investigation into both sides of our bloodline. Firstly, find out **who are they**? Secondly, find out **how they can be identified?** And lastly, find out **how dead relatives are able to have great influence in our lives today?**

e. WHO ARE THE HIDDEN STRANGERS?

The sin principle entered into the human genome when Adam and Eve violated a direct command.[66] It was transferred to them directly from Hasatan. At a point in eternity past, when Hasatan was called **Morning Star, son of the dawn**, iniquity was first found in him. The Amplified Version of the Bible states, *'You were blameless in your ways from the day you were created until iniquity and guilt were found in you.'*[67] There was a point in eternity past when this bright anointed keruv (cherub) was blameless.

If G-d is Spirit, His Kingdom must of necessity be spiritual. Therefore, from a human perspective, G-d's Kingdom is *unseen*. The Kingdom of Light is hidden from the children of Darkness. Aspects of G-d's Kingdom can even be hidden from children of the Light, just because the darkened areas of their lives have not yet become illuminated by G-d's Word.[68] Hasatan **introduced iniquity** into the human genome, which *set in motion* the process of mutation. How was Hasatan able to do this? Firstly, he removed his worship from *El'Elyon*, to himself; corrupting his beauty and splendour, which produced iniquity **in him**. Secondly, Hasatan caused Adam and Eve to become disconnected

---

[66] Romans 5: 12-14, 18, 19
[67] Ezekiel 28: 15 AMP
[68] Ephesians 5: 13 AMP

from G-d's order, by corrupting their innocence.[69] This mutation caused *immediate rebellion* to erupt within the consciousness of Adam and Eve; which in turn, gave way to the reign of Darkness from within. This was how Hasatan stole Adam's inheritance. **Adam gave up his rights** to have *'dominion and authority'* over the Earth. Heaven belongs to *ADONAI*, but the earth he has given to humankind.[70]

> [130] Your words are a doorway that lets in light, giving understanding to the thoughtless.
>
> **Tehillim (Psalm) 119: 130**

According to Romans chapter five and verse twelve, '…it was **through one individual** that sin entered the world…' If sin entered the world through one individual's lawbreaking, this tells me that Adam's sin affected the human bloodline. Sin, lawbreaking and rebellion was passed on from *generation to generation* in the human bloodline. The Kingdom of Darkness was planted in **the first Adam** as a seed that continued to grow until the tree of the knowledge of good and evil became a system that ruled the human race from within and without.

Until you speak to Adam in person, **you couldn't begin to imagine what it felt like to have been a completely**

---

[69] B'resheet 3: 4 - 6
[70] Tehillim 115: 16

innocent, blameless and sinless human being. Moreover, because you were born in sin, you will never experience the type of separation Adam felt when iniquity was first introduced into his system. After Adam, every person was born guilty; born with a consciousness of sin and a tendency to rebel against G-d's order. What is this tendency to rebel? It is the rebellious tendencies of evil spirits, who are the offspring of a union between the heavenly Watchers and the daughters of men. (see chapter One).

Because evil spirits are related to mankind, **they share** the lives of every individual from the time they are born, to the time they die, if they are not detected. **They develop** alongside the bloodline to which they are assigned, in order to share human life as an infant, a toddler, an adolescence, a teenager, an adult, a parent, a grandparent and a great grandparent. What am I saying? I am saying that these hidden strangers aim to develop in family units, for the purposes of establishing three-generational satanic agendas.

f.   IDENTIFY THE HIDDEN STRANGER

After David committed adultery with Bat-Sheva (Bathsheba), he realized that *his problem was iniquity.* In the book of Tehillim chapter fifty-one, *David's prayer of repentance included the iniquities of his bloodline.* A hidden stranger emerged, who was assigned to Rachav (Rahab) the prostitute. David didn't know Rachav personally, however, at a time when kings were supposed to go to war, **the hidden**

stranger assigned to the life of Rachav, came to the forefront. The hidden stranger attached to the life of Rachav, was aware that it could be annihilated in the fourth generation - David's generation. **David's hidden stranger fought and won the battle to stay in his bloodline.** As a result of David's sin with Bat-Sheva, the hidden stranger attached to the life of Rachav, continued to have a firm hold on David's bloodline. David's offspring bore the consequences of his actions.

A Major Strongman shows up whenever a blood relative reaches a certain level in their development of intimacy with G-d. Intimacy with G-d threatens the enemy. The Strongman who was attached to Rachav when she was living, felt threatened because David carried the authority of a king. *A fourth-generation ancestral spirit*, carries a high level of authority in the Kingdom of Darkness.

David's great grandmother Rachav, the harlot who hid the two spies sent to Yericho (Jericho), a fourth-generational blood relative to David, was responsible for creating a massive weakness in his bloodline. Rachav's adulterous lifestyle affected her descendants, which in turn, caused David to have *a weakness towards the same type of sin*. Like Ya'akov who wrestled with G-d all night until daybreak, David's time had come to close the door on *a major four-generational iniquitous pattern* introduced by his great grandmother. By the fourth generation, an iniquitous pattern can be completely annihilated in the bloodline. I believe that the person G-d chooses for the task of breaking generational iniquity in their bloodline, can be born in the third or fourth generation.

Among his many other gifts, David was a born Worshipping Warrior, with the anointing and authority to overcome a four-generational weakness. David's *set time* arrived, when king's go out to war, however, he missed his appointed time.

> [1] In the spring, at the time when kings go out to war, David sent out Yo'av, his servants who were with him and all Isra'el. They ravaged the people of 'Amon and laid siege to Rabbah. But David stayed in Yerushalayim. [2] Once, after his afternoon nap, David got up from his bed and went strolling on the roof of the king's palace. From the roof he saw a woman bathing, who was very beautiful. [3] David made inquiries about the woman and was told that she was Bat-Sheva the daughter of Eli'am, the wife of Uriyah the Hitti. [4] David sent messengers to get her, and she came to him, and he went to bed with her (for she had been purified from her uncleanness). Then she returned to her house. [5] The woman conceived; and she sent a message to David, "I am pregnant."

Sh'mu'el Bet (2 Samuel) 11: 1-5

The thing that struck me when reading verse one in the above Scripture text, is that David did not enquire of the L-rd as to whether he should stay behind or go to war. On many other occasions, David asked the L-rd if he should go to war and whether he would win. On this occasion, kings were supposed to go out to war and David was a king. Why didn't David enquire of the L-rd about his decision to stand down? I believe, *a four-generational spiritual relative seized the opportunity,* to come out of hiding to secure her place in the bloodline. Why? Because these strangers of iniquity recognized that the threat to their annihilation was in the fourth generation.

Had David gone out to war in the company of the other kings, I believe he would have successfully closed the door on generational sin and iniquity in his bloodline. **David's missed opportunity allowed the four-generational spirit of the harlot that was attached to his great grandmother to surface.** The spirit of the prostitute emerged in full force at a time when David was *exposed and vulnerable.* David's absence from a war with the kings, meant that *he had no weapons of war in his hand;* he let his guard down and was **defenceless against a relative he knew nothing about.**

Remember, Ya'akov was the head of his clan and therefore, like a king. As the head of his clan, Ya'akov recognized that he was authorized to go to war, in order to close the door on generational iniquity in is bloodline. *As a king and a warrior, David failed to meet the challenge on behalf of his bloodline.* The events that unfolded during *David's displacement* was the revelation of a four-generational prostitute spirit that was attach to his great grandmother. The spirit of the harlot put David in bondage whilst waging a warfare to remain in the bloodline. **A strong spirit of lust overpowered David, causing him to crave for another man's wife.** Isn't this how a harlot behaves? A harlot spirit, always takes that which belongs to another person. **Though Rachav is no more, the spirit that was assigned to her while she was alive, overpowered David, causing him to commit adultery with another man's wife.** *David was rendered powerless to a four-generational strongman, who revealed himself to David for the first time.*

David eventually realized that he had come face-to-face with the stranger that was attached to his great grandmother Rachav. When the prophet Natan, uncovered David's sin, David understood that he had failed to close the door on generational sin and iniquity in his bloodline. He was told that his family would experience backlash because of his actions.

> [9] So why have you shown such contempt for the word of *ADONAI* and done what I see as evil? **You murdered** Uriyah the Hitti with the sword and **took his wife as your own wife;** you put him to death with the sword of the people of 'Amon. [10] Now therefore, **the sword will never leave your house** – because you have shown contempt for me and taken the wife of Uriyah the Hitti as your own wife. [11] Here is what *ADONAI* says: 'I will generate evil against you out of your own household. **I will take your wives before your very eyes and give them to your neighbour; he will go to bed with your wives, and everyone will know about it.** [12] For you did it secretly, but I will do this before all Isra'el in broad daylight. [13] David said to Natan, "I have sinned against *ADONAI*." Natan said to David, "*ADONAI* also has taken away your sin. You will not die. [14]

However, because by this act you have so greatly blasphemed *ADONAI*, the child born to you must die."

Sh'mu'el Bet (2 Samuel) **12: 9 - 14**

David had blood on his hands; he *intentionally* murdered Uriyah by sending him to the frontline. King David *attempted to cover up* the fact that he slept with Uriyah's wife. This was a calculated, cold-blooded murderous act.

Amnon's rape of his half-sister Tamar and Avshalom's (Absalom's) murder of Amnon begin David's inter-family troubles, which Natan (Nathan) the prophet announced when pronouncing judgment on David for his sin with Bat-Sheva and the murder of Uriyah: "The sword will never leave your house" (cf. 12: 10).[71]

g. YOUR DEAD RELATIVES HAVE INFLUENCE IN YOUR LIVES TODAY

You are responsible for your own sins and for allowing the iniquities of your forefathers to have influence in your life. David was being strongly influenced by *the spirit of murder and lust*. Though David was fully aware that his intentions put a gulf between him and his G-d, *he made the decision* to take another man's wife and murder her husband, regardless. You must endeavour to guard your heart, for out of it flows the issues of life. If you have found yourself in the wrong place at the wrong time, beware! If you are a leader

---

[71] from the footnote in Sh'mu'el Bet 13, p. 390, CJB

and have great influence, beware! The hidden strangers in your bloodline, will show themselves, especially if they are threatened or served noticed.

It is time for believers in the Messiah, to take a stand against generational sin and iniquity in their bloodline, and they must do it on purpose. A hidden stranger will feel threatened when **the logos Word** becomes **the rhema Word**. When G-d's Word becomes a living reality, the hidden strangers in the bloodline will surface because *revelation knowledge* will **burn them out** like the fires of Hell.

If you stop feeding on your external environment, the hidden strangers in your bloodline will become unsettled. This can only happen if you have made **a decision** to *immerse yourself in G-d's Word*. The hidden strangers in your bloodline have an appetite for the world, which is why *starvation* brings them to the surface in protest. The *rhema* word will destroy everything the hidden strangers are accustomed to feeding on. You must stay in the Word until they turn to ashes!

> [29] "Isn't my word like fire," asks ADONAI, like a hammer shattering rocks?
>
> **Yirmeyahu (Jeremiah) 23: 29**

h. THE DRUG DEALER - TRAFFICKER

A Drug Dealer is no different from a local witchdoctor who supplies drugs or uses it as *a form of manipulation*. Those who have an addiction to illegal substances or prescription pills are *in an ongoing covenant with the Devil*.

i. THE WITCHDOCTOR

A witchdoctor is a practitioner who *mixes herbs and potions for the purposes of 'casting-a-spell.'* Witchdoctors have sold their souls to the devil, in return for power. As agents of darkness, they have delegated demonic power and authority to cast spells. Using their *craft*, and the *seducing spirits* assigned to them, they will *take advantage of a person's weakness to drugs*. The witchdoctor's place of residence, serves as *a portal* through which demonic spirits are given license to enter those who step into their territory. Witchdoctors are assisted by *household servants* called, **Familiar spirits**.

Question: "What are familiar spirits?"

Answer: The word *familiar* is from the Latin word *familiaris;* meaning a "**household servant,**" and is intended to express the idea that sorcerers had spirits as their servants ready to obey their commands. Those attempting to contact the dead, even to this day, usually have some sort of **spirit guide** who communicates with them. These are *familiar spirits.* **Familiar spirits and guides are under the control of their master, Satan.** *They influence* people to spread lies and deceit in order to thwart the Kingdom of G-d. **To**

knowingly open oneself to the work of demons is an evil thing: "There must not be found among you anyone who makes his son or daughter pass through fire, a diviner, a soothsayer, an enchanter, a sorcerer, a spell-caster, a consulter of ghosts or spirits, or a necromancer. For whoever does these things is detestable to ADONAI" (D'varim/Deuteronomy 18: 10-12a).

Some avenues through which demons or "familiar spirits" can gain entrance into a person's life are divination, transcendental meditation, visualization, necromancy, witchcraft, *drugs and alcohol*. These are all activities that believers are exhorted to avoid. Instead, we are to be filled with the Ruach HaKodesh, with love, with joy, and with the fullness of life that comes from Yeshua HaMashiach. We are also to be on guard, "for we are **not** **struggling against human beings,** but against the rulers, authorities and cosmic *powers governing this darkness*, against the *spiritual forces of evil* in the heavenly realm" (Ephesians 6: 12).[72]

The Greek word for 'witchcraft' is called, *pharmakeia* and means, *medication* (pharmacy), *magic sorcery, a drug*, i.e., *spell-giving potion, a druggist* (pharmacist) *or poisoner*, i.e., *magician: - sorcerer*. **Any person who has formed an addiction to prescribed medication or mind-altering drugs have knowingly or unknowingly entered into a covenant with** *Hasatan*. Illegal substances are addictive and represents what an addict treasures most. An addict will do almost anything to feed their addiction; they live for their next 'fix.'

---

[72] https://www.gotquestions.org/familiar-spirits.html

---

j. CONCLUSION

According to Mattityahu chapter six and verse twenty-one, our heart is attached to our treasure. Whenever drugs are purchased, buyers offer themselves to be sacrificed on a satanic altar. ***To Purchase drugs is to strike a bargin with Hasatan for your soul;*** just as the people of Yisra'el did when they worshiped ***Ba'al*** (the god worshiped by the Kena'ani). The Hebrew word for ***Ba'al*** means, *to be master, to marry, to have dominion over, a husband, owner, lord.*

Table 6. Five Demonic Spirits and their Definitions

1. Familiar	*medium, consulting the dead, drugs, spiritualist, false prophet, an associate,* ***a household servant.***
2. Divination	*warlock or witch, fortune-teller,* ***drugs,*** *hypnotist, magic, horoscopes, zodiacs, rebellion, sorcery, clairvoyance, prediction, (soothsaying), alcohol*
3. Bondage	*addictions, bondage to sin, phobias, captivity to Hasatan, compulsive sin,* ***slavery, enslavement,*** *servitude, oppression, subjugation, subjection, exploitation, persecution, detention, domination*
4. Fear	***torment,*** *intimidation, instability, doubtfulness, domination, destructive, disempower, fright, terror, alarm, horror,* ***dread,*** *trepidation, panic, fright*
5. Deception	*cheat, lying, trickery, fraud,* ***cunning,*** *deviousness, artfulness, pretence*

10 *Hold On to Your Liberty*

Liberation means holding on to the freedom that you have gained. Imagine going out to wage a bloody warfare, in order to secure a large piece of territory that once belonged to your family. After the 'high' of gaining a triumphant victory over the enemies who stole your family inheritance, you may begin to feel a bit deflated when it's all over. Depending on how vast the territory is, after a little while, you may even start to wonder whether you are able manage the size of your inheritance.

Though you may be the inheritor of a territory, it doesn't mean that you have mastery over that territory. You see, **winning a territory and having mastery over it are two different things**. Your *development within* the territory you won, depends on *the size* of the territory. A small territory will take less time for you to master it, whereas, the larger territory will take a longer time for you to become the master over it.

a. KINGDOM CULTURE

The culture of G-d's Kingdom must be installed within your self-life; this is how G-d originally intended us to develop in relation to Him. G-d planted a Garden and gave Man the job to **tend**, **guard** and **keep** it. G-d hardwired humankind to *cultivate* their relationship with Him, so that it wouldn't be a one-sided form of communication, but a one-to-one, purposeful interaction. I believe this kind of relationship with G-d is **the real shalom**. When a born-again believer develops an intimate relationship with *ADONAI*, oneness is achieved. This oneness with *ADONAI* is what attracts G-d Himself to come and commune with us. You see, as long as, Adam focused on *staying connected* with the Garden of Eden, G-d would always personally show up.

b. EDEN – THE ENVIRONMENT OF G-D'S SON

During the writing of my doctoral dissertation on True Governmental Worship, the Ruach HaKodesh revealed to me, that the Garden of Eden was a representation of the Second Person of the Tri-unity. G-d showed His affection for humankind by placing Adam within the environment or the territory of His Son. Why did G-d do this? He did this so that Adam could cultivate a sonship relationship with His Creator and get to know Him as Father. Before sin, G-d gave Adam this order: *"You may freely eat from every tree in the garden, except the tree of the knowledge of good and evil. You are not to eat from it, because on the day that you eat from it, it will become certain that you will die."*[73]

---

[73] B'resheet 2: 16, 17

c. AN AUTHENTIC UNION WITH G-D
IS ACHIEVED IN HIS SON

G-d gave Adam freedom to grow and develop within His command, with the exception of one commandment. Before *the fall*, Adam had not yet developed an understanding of death and separation from G-d, nor how to maintain a lifestyle of unbroken union with G-d.

However, Adam did have some experience of freedom, albeit short-lived. Adam learned the harsh realities of what it really meant to be separated from union with G-d, because of his disobedience. G-d's intentions for Man's growth and development was supposed to be conducted *within* the environment of His Beloved Son – The Garden of Eden (Gan Eden).

This brings me to the point where David resonates with the separation Adam felt after he broke covenant with G-d: *"True, I was born guilty, was a sinner from the moment my mother conceived me."*[74] The Amplified Version of the Bible says it this way: *"Behold, I was brought forth in a state of iniquity; my mother was sinful who conceived me and I too am sinful."* Here, David acknowledges **his own sin** and **the sins of his own bloodline**. There is also a possibility that David could have been making reference to Adam and Eve's lawbreaking.

---

[74] Tehillim 51: 5

---

d. TRUE FREEDOM IN THE MESSIAH

It is clear to see that from the beginning, G-d gave humankind freedom of choice. Adam's freedom to eat from every tree in the garden, far outweighed the one exception. G-d intended for Adam to grow in his understanding of *how to passionately guard his union with G-d.*

The tree of the knowledge of good and evil was planted in the garden, in order to give humankind a sense of observing G-d's boundary line. The tree of the knowledge of good and evil served as a daily reminder to Adam and Eve, that choosing to obey G-d would preserve shalom.

e. SHALOM – THE MISSING FACTOR

G-d's Shalom is the missing factor in the *'olam hazeh*. Until we come face-to-face with our own sins and that of our bloodline, we can mistakenly think that we are good people. Seriously, at some point in our lives, we all have to take a long look at ourselves in the mirror and acknowledge that we were born in sin and moulded in iniquity. If you can make the decision to take time out of your busy lives to spend time alone with G-d, He will show you who you really are.

A face-to-face encounter with G-d will reveal the hidden strangers who inhabit the bloodlines in both sides of your family. Like *Adam, Moshe, Ya'akov and David*, we usually become aware of our iniquities when we have committed a sin. Only then do we realize that we have an underlying tendency or weakness to sin. Our disobedience highlights the absence of *the G-d kind of liberty* and the G-d kind of shalom!

f. WORLDLY BELIEVERS

If you are a worldly-minded believer, your continued love affair with the *'olam hazeh* is a type of incarceration. You'll never realize that you are still a slave, if you keep feeding on the *'olam hazeh*. Isn't it just like the god of this world to make you think that you are free to come and go as you please? Only when you continue to look into the mirror of G-d's Word, will you begin to realize that you still have some areas of brokenness in your life that need to be fixed.

The inability to apply G-d's Word to your life indicates that you have an area of darkness your life. Wherever there is evidence of darkness, there is enslavement. A person in mental slavery, is not at liberty to obey G-d's orders, let alone apply them to their lives. Your inability to be obedient to a specific command from G-d, shows that you are in a bondage that relates to that specific command.

The strongman assigned to keep you in bondage, must first be bound, so that you can to be liberated. It is not unusual for a person to be born again and still have a bondage to sin, in one area or the other. Sin cannot take possession of a true believer because the *Ruach HaKodesh* resides in the regenerated spirit. However, if the mind is not being continually renewed by G-d's Word, *born again doubters* will remain enslaved to sin because their minds have not been liberated from the dominion of darkness.[75]

g. KEEP A CHECK ON YOURSELF

As believers of *ADONAI* living in this world, we all need to have **regular spiritual detoxing,** to make sure that our relationship with G-d has not been compromised. Keep tabs on *the source* of your ideas and opinions. Keep a close check on yourself, to see whether you are walking in the **spiritual liberation,** that the Messiah purchased for you. Living or abiding in the Messiah, is to live and abide within the boundary lines of G-d's shalom. This is how G-d conducted His relationship with Man before the *fall.*

> This **"spiritual liberation"** comes through the ministry of the word into people's lives. Yeshua declared the grand reality: "You are truly my disciples if you abide in My word; and you shall know the truth, and the truth shall set you free" (Yochanan 8: 31 – 32). The key word here is "abide" – Yeshua tells His followers precisely in what discipleship consists: abiding in His word. Yeshua said He is "the truth and the life" (Yochanan 14: 6). **When people consistently ingest the word of G-d into their lives, it goes to work effectively in their hearts, liberating them from that which has bound them.** Remember, "the word of G-d is

---

[75] Romans 12: 1, 2

living and active" (Messianic Jews 4: 12) ... it is "the sword of the Spirit (Ephesians 6: 17) ... the Spirit guides believers "into the fullness of the truth" (Yochanan 16: 13). The apostle Sha'ul says, "Where the Spirit of the Lord is, there is freedom" (2 Corinthians 3: 17) G-d's word is unique and powerful; it is not merely the religious words of men. Through the execution stake, *the Messiah brought about our redemption* (which is liberation in the stronger sense of the word); it has freed us from the most radical evil – the tyrants of sin and death. The result of sin is guilt, shame, alienation, depression, emptiness, loneliness, pain and death. Yeshua taught us to pray, "Deliver us from evil;" it is here we petition the Father to act with power over evil in our daily lives. *Bob Hoekstra*, the son of chaplain Ray, says: "Those who earnestly get into the word become gloriously liberated" (Hoekstra). **The truth of the Messiah is the only path to spiritual freedom – it delivers us from the debilitating chains of evil and darkness.** Someone once described it this way:

> *Our selfish ways imprison us – we cry out to be free;*
> *But if we will obey G-d's Word, we'll find true liberty.*
> *(Yoder)*[76]

h. MENTAL SLAVERY

Yes, it is true that G-d paid a high price to redeem us from sin and its effects; in that, even when we were dead because of our acts of disobedience, he brought us to life along with the Messiah – it is *by his grace* that we have been delivered.

---

[76] http://www.thetransformedsoul.com/additional-studies/spiritual-life-studies/spiritual-liberation

By doing this, *Yeshua HaMashiach* changed **our position** (in relation to sin), and **our direction** (in relation to purpose).

G-d exchanged your life and your status for the life and status of His Son – how awesome is that? You didn't have to do a thing except believe and accept His wonderful gift of salvation, which came through the sacrifice made by His only begotten Son, *Yeshua HaMashiach.*

According to Yoder, writer of the excerpt on P. 117: '...*the Messiah brought about your redemption, which is liberation in the stronger sense of the word; it has freed you from the most radical evil – the tyrants of sin and death.*' G-d did His part to liberate you from sin and death, however, your covenant relationship means that there is a part that you must play, in order to **enforce the power of covenant** in your life.[77]

You are also required to pay the price of going through 'a type of death'; which is *the dying to self.* If you fail to do this, sin and iniquity will continue to go *undetected* in your mind, will and emotions – your soul. Your soul, is where the spiritual warfare takes place. The sooner you understand this the closer you will get to *soul liberation.* **Your powers** are embedded in your soul. G-d hardwired you with *the powers* of mind, will and emotion. When G-d's supernatural power is applied to the powers He gave you, you will be able to walk in dominion and authority.

---

[77] Romans 8: 17

> ³ For although we do live in the world, we do not wage war in a worldly way; ⁴ because the weapons we use to wage war are not worldly. On the contrary, they have God's power for demolishing strongholds. **We demolish arguments** ⁵ and **every arrogance** that <u>raises</u> <u>itself up</u> **against the knowledge of God**; we take every thought captive and make it obey the Messiah. ⁶ And when you have become completely obedient, then we will be ready to punish every act of disobedience.

2 Corinthians 10: 3 - 6

This passage of Scripture is telling us that we are to use the anointed Word as a weapon to demolish mind-sets that cause internal rebellion. Behind every stronghold is a strongman who is the imposter responsible for *the war of words* that *argue* in defence of self. When you confront the truth of G-d's Word, the truth will confront the lies hiding in the darkened areas of your life. **Until the lie is replaced by the Truth, G-d will not entrust you to represent Him.**

i.   WHAT IS A CURSE?

In the Bible, three different Hebrew words are translated as "curse." The most common is a ritualistic formulation which described as "cursed" those who violate community standards defined by G-d and tradition. Slightly less common is a word used to invoke evil against anyone who violates a contract or oath. A curse is the opposite of a blessing: whereas a blessing is a pronouncement of good fortune because one is initiated into G-d's plans, a curse is a pronouncement of ill fortune because on opposes G-d's plans.[78] A curse entered the human race, as a result of rebellion against G-d; it gave the devil the licence to damage and deface the image of G-d in you. Being born in sin and conceived in iniquity is the result of the curse brought about by one Man's disobedient act in the Garden of Eden. Our crimes have separated us from our G-d and our sins have hidden his face from us. Separation from G-d will expose you to curses. I don't believe that the devil would have been able to articulate or invoke curses without the existence of *a standard of righteousness*; which produces fruits of righteousness. The fruit of righteousness is blessings.

> [12] For our crimes multiply before you, ours sins testify against us; for our crimes are present with us; and our sins, we know them well: [13] rebelling and denying ADONAI, turning away from following our God, talking about oppression and revolt, uttering lies which our hearts have conceived.

> **Yesha'yahu (Isaiah) 59: 12, 13**

A curse opens the door for demons to enter the life of a person, and creates the right environment for demons to feel at home. A curse will rest on the first, second, third and fourth generations of a bloodline.

---

[78] https://www.thoughtco.com/what-is-a-curse-248646

j. IDENTIFY CURSES

A curse occurs through a break in communion with G-d. Every sin committed, attracts a curse and creates the legal ground for demons to operate.[79] Sin accommodates curses, sometimes released through negative words. A curse is the consequence of a sin, such as disobedience; though the curse is visible, the sin that caused the curse remains *invisible*. The specific sins committed by your forefathers may never be known to you, however, the curse produced by their sins can be visible in your life and the lives of your living relatives.

> [7] Our ancestors sinned and no longer exist; we bear the weight of their guilt. [8] We are ruled by slaves, and there is no one to save us from their power.
>
> **Eikhah (Lamentations) 5: 7, 8**

Curses can lie undetected in the soul of a believer, until they stumble across G-d's Word. A threat to the existence of a curse will cause the *familial spirit* attached, to become exposed. The *familial spirit* has replaced the personality embedded in the mind, will and emotion of an individual.

A curse is the culture that supports the demonic personality's thought processes, decisions, feelings, habits, *patterns of behaviour* and traditions. **A behavioural pattern is a repetitive mode of the action.** A *cyclical pattern* is one way

---

[79] B'resheet 4: 6, 7; 1Kefa 5: 8

of identifying a curse. If the demon is representing you, it means you are bound and rendered powerless to be your own authentic self. It never ceases to amaze me, how as believers, we continue to behave like imposters instead of sons and daughters of *El 'Elyon* (G-d Most-High). A person who has been truly converted, can still give the devil legal ground in their lives.

k. MIKVEH – A DAILY IMMERSION IN G-D'S WORD

The biggest threat to the enemy of your soul is the revelation of G-d's Word. Demonic influence is the main reason why believers rebel against studying G-d's Word, even though they confess to having a deep love for G-d.[80] I'll never forget the time, some twenty-two years ago now, when I was having an intimate moment in G-d's Presence: I said, *"L-rd, I really do love you"*. His immediate response was: *"If you really love Me, obey my commandment!"* At the time, I remembered not being at all surprised at His response. I recognized G-d's voice because I recognized His words from my many years of studies. When you make the decision to become a *talmidim* (lifelong student of G-d's Word), you will begin to hear and recognize when His speaks. In contrast, G-d will also speak in a way that the spiritually immature will understand. G-d knows how to communicate His words to

---

[80] Yochanan 14: 23

each and every one of His precious children. Take a look at
the woman of Shomron (Samaria), she knew nothing about
True Worship. Her worship was not *heart worship*; it was
not relational, it was ritualistic.[81]

1. HEARING G-D'S WORD
IN A THREE-DIMENSIONAL WAY

The woman from Shomron did not realize that *men* had
taken the placed G-d and Father in her heart. As long as she
held on to her *men-idols*, True Worship would remain elusive
to her. Yeshua confronted a woman in search of something
life-changing. She was a sinner who knew nothing about
True Worship, yet Yeshua was able to expose her **heart
problem** and show her how to experience true liberation.

The woman from Shomron heard and understood what was
being communicated to her because for the first time, she
was hearing a Man who could communicate in three
dimensions: *spiritual, mental* and *physical*.[82] The woman from
Shomron had a discourse with the Word, which,
immediately produced radical changes in her life. Her
liberation was so radical that it overflowed into the lives of
her towns people. The Father will not speak to you from a
distance, He is saying to you, "Give Me a drink of water."

---

[81] Yochanan 4: 22
[82] Yochanan 4: 5 – 25; Messianic Jews 4: 12

m. HEREDITARY CURSES

Hereditary curses are transferred through the bloodline. They install themselves in us, through parents or ancestors who gave curses the legal right to enter the lives of their descendants:

Table 7: Some Hereditary Curses

1.Rebellion against G-d (Sh'mu'el Alef 15: 23a)	*For rebellion is like the sin of sorcery, stubborn-ness like the crime of idolatry.*
2.Witchcraft (D'varim 18: 10-11)	*There must not be found among you anyone who makes his son or daughter pass through fire, a diviner, a soothsayer, an enchanter, a sorcerer, a spell-caster, a consulter of ghosts or spirits, or necromancer.*
3.Idolatry (Sh'mot 20: 3 – 5)	*You are to have no other gods before me. You are not to make for yourselves a carved image or any kind of representation of anything in heaven above, on the earth beneath or in the water below the shoreline. You are not to bow down to them or serve them; for I ADONAI your G-d, am a jealous G-d, punishing the children for the sins of the parents to the third and fourth generation of those who hate me.*
4.Adultery (Mishlei 6: 32)	*He who commits adultery lacks sense; he who does it, destroys himself.*
5.Prostitution (1 Corinthians 6:18)	*Run from sexual immorality! Every other sin a person commits, is outside the body, but the fornicator sins against his own body.*
6.Lies (Ephesians 4: 25)	*Therefore, stripping off falsehood, let everyone speak truth with his neighbor, because we are intimately related to each other as parts of a body.*

n. VOLUNTARY CURSES

Voluntary curses occur when a person makes a **decision** to sin; like choosing to cast a spell, choosing to commit adultery, choosing to take drugs or choosing to get involved in prostitution.

o. CURSES OVER NATIONS

All nations have opened the door to curses. In most nations, colonization gave license to a plethora of curses such as idolatry, witchcraft, satanic worship, prostitution and more.[83] History records many First World Nations as having robbed many Third World Nations of their natural resources and conscripted the natives to becoming their slave population. Many First World Nations are guilty of committing piracy against unsuspecting natives of foreign lands, who openly welcomed them, not knowing that they harboured evil intentions towards them.

Natives of Third World countries were stripped of their inheritance through the practices of sexual abuse, physical abuse and acts of genocide. This was how many Third World countries were dominated by the West. Consequently, many of those who have come to the West, from Third World Nations, are known to have *chunks of their history missing.*

---

[83] D'varim 18: 10–14; 1 Corinthians 6: 15-16; Revelation 6: 8

The slave owners who fathered children to slave women, have refuse to acknowledge them as a blood relative because slaves were viewed as commodities, not human beings. For hundreds of years, these atrocities have been swept under the carpet of Western governments. In the bloodlines of slave owners however, lies a hatred towards all descendants of slaves. Western societies, in particular, have an underlying evil called: '**Institutional Racism**.' Twenty First Century Britain is well known for embracing all faiths and as a result, *idol worship has become prevalent.*

p. TRAUMA INDUCED CURSES

Some demons enter through a trauma that occurred during infancy, adolescence or adulthood. Traumatic experiences leave their traits in our attitudes, even when the trauma is known to be a historical factor in our bloodline.

Traumas can be caused by: *rejection, sexual abuse, violence, fear, fights, accidents, abandonment, a lack of love, harsh words, drugs, absent parents, divorce, fornication, adultery, promiscuity and abortion.* Like the woman from Shomron (Samaria) liberation will come when you *decide to confront* the Son of Man. You can only find a cure from a trauma suffered, through the Execution Stake upon which Yeshua hung.[84]

---

[84] Galatians 3: 13

q. CURSES PRODUCED BY OUR WORDS

Words spoken, are like seeds that are sown in the mind of the hearer. As time passes by, the seeds sown will come to fruition. Words can build us up or destroy us. Our words are responsible for starting wars, divisions, deaths, hatred and disasters.[85] By our words, we will be justified or condemned.[86] The pronouncement of curses over a person's life will eventually cause that person to become dysfunctional. Like David, let us ask the L-rd to guard our lips.

> [3] Set a guard, ADONAI, over my mouth; keep watch at the door of my lips.

Tehillim 141: 3

People who indulge in **gossiping** and **mocking others**, are *creating an environment* for a curse to enter the lives of those who may have an inferiority complex. *An undisciplined tongue can cause irreconcilable damage,* which only Yeshua is able to repair. Many parents have made negative confessions over the lives of their children; calling their sons *a sissy* and their daughters *butch*, or telling them they are *worthless idles* and *good for nothing*. Sadly, these negative words have brought the lives of our sons and daughters to a quick end.

---

[85] Mishlei (Proverbs) 15: 1; Ya'akov (James) 3: 7-12
[86] Mattityahu 12: 36, 37

Since *life and death is in the power of the tongue,* we must endeavour to *counteract the effects of death-loaded words* by speaking words that are life-giving and restorative.[87] Remember, **every word is a seed** that can, potentially, give demons the legal ground to share your life.

r. CURSES THAT ENTER THROUGH
THE DOORWAY OF LEADERSHIP

Curses that are permitted to enter through the doorway of **ministerial sins** can be established in family groups, that extend to the third and fourth generations. The **sin of adultery and fornication** are prevalent curses that have taken root within many ministries. The nature of this type of sin, in particular, prevents members of the Messianic Community from engaging in True Worship. *The sins of adultery and fornication represent a counterfeit worship.*

Counterfeit worship is a perversion of True Worship. It was the sin of adultery and fornication that kept the Woman from Shomron chained to a perversion of worship. Her worship of men, kept her imprisoned to the curses of guilt and shame. Many ministries **cover their guilt and shameful acts** with strict religious observances and traditions. A Religious person will observe *acts of righteousness,* in order to cover up a guilty conscience. Adam and Eve did the same thing; they *covered their shame and nakedness with the fig leaves* they had

---

[87] Mishlei 18: 21

---

sewn together. Their guilt and shame caused them to create a covering.[88] *Traditions house our guilty acts, when they are employed as outward works of self-righteousness.*[89]

In order to expose and eliminate guilt and shameful acts from amongst the Messianic Community, leaders must take a stand against these unclean spirits by open confession and repentance of sin. Call them out!! **Ministries can suffer from generational curses** therefore, leaders must guide the Messianic Community to *humble themselves, pray, seek* G-d's Face and turn from their evil ways. *True repentance will cause G-d to hear from heaven, forgive sin and heal* the whole community.[90]

> [27] You have heard that our fathers were told, '**Do not commit adultery.**' [28] But I tell you that a man who even looks at a woman with the purpose of lusting after her has already committed adultery with her in his heart. [29] If your right eye makes you sin, gouge it out and throw it away! Better that you should lose one part of you than have your whole body thrown into Gei-Hinnom. [30] And if your right hand makes you sin, cut it off and throw it away! Better that you should lose one part of you than have your whole body thrown into Gei-Hinnom.
>
> **Mattityahu 5: 27-30**

---

[88] B'resheet 3: 1-7

[89] Yesha'yahu (Isaiah) 64: 6

[90] Divrei-Hayamim Bet (2 Chronicles) 7: 14

---

s. CHOOSE BLESSINGS OR CURSES

You are a free moral agent because G-d hard-wired you to have freedom of choice. On a daily basis, *you can choose whether to walk in the blessings of ADONAI or walk in the curses.* If you choose to have an affair with curses, your life will soon become dysfunctional.[91] **G-d urges us to choose blessings** because He created us in His own image and established *laws* for our own protection. Choosing the curse is to step outside of G-d's protection. **Choosing to Observe** G-d's *mitzvot*, will cause you to *stand out* like a light on a hilltop.

> [1] "If you listen closely to what *ADONAI* your God says, observing and obeying all his *mitzvot* which I am giving you today, *ADONAI* your God will raise you high above all the nations on earth; [2] and all the following blessings will be yours in abundance – if you will do what *ADONAI* your God says ...
>
> [58] If you will not observe and obey all the words of this *Torah* that are written in this book, so that you will fear this glorious and awesome name, *ADONAI* your God; [59] then *ADONAI* will strike down you and your descendants with extraordinary plagues and severe sicknesses that go on and on.
>
> **D'varim 28: 1-2, 58-59**

In our daily walk with *ADONAI*, there should never be a trace of ambiguity. We must decide whether we are going to

---

[91] D'varim 11: 26-28

sell our souls to the god of the *'olam hazeh,* or live to please our heavenly Father. G-d does not get any pleasure out of lukewarm believers. The Word of G-d said that *the kind of person who is neither hot or cold would be spewed out of G-d's mouth.*[92] Your behaviour, translates as spiritual language that can be understood in G-d's Kingdom. As a child of G-d, you must become increasingly aware that **who you are today, is what you have been saying about yourself yesterday**.

I encourage you to feed on G-d's Word, in order to change your *thinking*, which will in turn change the way that you *speak*. The *'olam hazeh* is temporary, fleeting and fading away. Our sinful world produces curses that are sugar-coated because the god of this world wants you *addicted* to him. If you feed on the *'olam hazeh,* your life will become the product of curses. If you feed on G-d's life-giving Word, your life will become the product of G-d's blessings and your speech will be life-giving.

t. CONCLUSION

Be encouraged! The painful experiences that seem to follow you around can be broken in an instant. Familial curses can be broken over your life and the life of your descendants in an instant. Just one encounter with *Yeshua HaMashiach,* can change your life and your circumstances in a moment. **It is**

---

[92] Revelation 3: 16

---

not G-d's will for you to perish. It is time for you to be liberated from the generational curses that have plagued your bloodline.

If you want to be free, it is absolutely possible to experience freedom in **a face-to-face encounter with G-d**. I believe that by prayerfully allowing the Word to *confront the familial spirits attached to your bloodline*, **you will begin to experience acceleration and exponential growth** in your personal life, your marriage, your family and your ministry. **G-d is about to fast-track you into the purpose to which you were born**.

Many of you will be shocked and surprized at how G-d will open up the ancient doors in front of you. Your current position in ministry is not where you will always be. Up until now, the familial spirits in your bloodline have prevented you from moving into the territory assigned to you. Today, you are about to lay hold of the inheritance that was stolen from you, and on multiple levels too! **If you want to experience liberation, you cannot settle for mediocrity.** <u>I adjure you to stand to up and begin to put one foot in front of the other. It is time for you to lay hold of your liberty!</u>

11 *The Self Diagnostic Approach*

Whuen you have completed this book, whether as an individual or as a group, you are now ready to take the next step. The therapeutic benefits of this anointed teaching course will have caused you to recognize that **you have been chosen to take on the responsibility of closing the door on generational sin and iniquity in your bloodline**.

If you have been experiencing feelings of fear, nervousness or even thoughts that say: *'Do you know what? I am absolutely fine, I'm good, I don't need to be free because I'm a child of G-d.'* I want you to know that this is typically how hidden strangers in the bloodline cause you to think. They are partakers of your life; your thought processes, your decisions and your emotions.

a. DECIDE TO WIN THE BATTLE

If threatened, the hidden strangers will put up a fight to stay in your life. If you wish to *walk in a greater level of G-d's anointing,* you must learn how to tend, guard and keep the territory of your self-life. When you have decided to **leave no stone unturned** until the enemies of your soul have been driven out, the battle has already been won.

b. SELF DIAGNOSIS

Some people will have more of a heightened self-awareness about the symptoms they have, even **before** they start reading this book. Others will be made aware of their symptoms or dysfunctions, **after** having read this book. This course will enable you to embrace **a self-diagnostic approach**, and will provide you with the tools to critically analyse your symptoms. The aim is to **sensitively and prayerfully pull apart your symptoms** in order to study and clarify the component parts of your particular dysfunction. This is the teaching course. It is the diagnosis – analysis phase.

c. THE PROGNOSIS

After the *diagnosis and analysis phase*, we will support you through the *prognosis phase.* You will arrive at the correct prognosis by honesty and agreement. You will need the support and guidance of your spiritual leader, a person or persons who you have asked to stand with you. *"What will happen if no treatment is administered?"* The prognosis phase will clarify what is likely to happen with or without treatment. Treatment has pre-conditions and consequential conditions. It would be unreasonable e.g., to expect transformation in a day, because the process may take a week, a month or a year.

The Consultant's or Leader's Prognosis about what is likely to happen, even with treatment, is important. This prognosis guides them to establish a realistic regime of treatment and solution. It is the basis of the prescription and or recommendation from the Consultant or the Leader about what needs to be done in order to bring about wholeness and wellness. **The prescription states** which elements of the symptoms, (the personality, the habits, the emotional makeup) need to be actually removed, or need to be *reassigned, repositioned* or *reconfigured.*

d. SELF ANALYSIS

The work of the Consultant or Worship Leader is to *sensitively and prayerfully*, put the component parts that have been observed and the diagnosis, back together again. This reordering is known as *synthesizing*, which means to **create a solution** or **create a new condition** or **create a new structure;** an *assembling* and *reassembling* of the component parts in a new way.

e. CULTIVATE YOUR GARDEN

The P'ni-El Therapy course is structured to support each person to return to the Garden of Eden. The Garden of Eden is the environment of G-d's Son; it is the place where G-d meets with us. The perfect place where G-d will come to have fellowship with you, is within the grounds of a soul that has been cultivated by His Word. In the beginning, *G-d* *intentionally planted a Garden* so that He could have fellowship and intimacy with humankind. It is your responsibility to *replicate that Garden in your mind, will and emotions* (your soul) by renewing your mind. A mind that is renewed by G-d's Word will become the Garden where the Presence of G-d will not be limited because it is the grounds or territory that is based on His Son.

f. THE TERMS OF AN AGREEMENT BETWEEN G-D AND MAN

The Word of G-d **is** the Garden of Eden environment; the grounds and the terms upon which G-d will meet with you. In the book of B'resheet you will notice that G-d first planted a Garden, and afterwards placed man in it, to tend, guard and keep it.[93] In a Twenty-First Century World, we can choose to meet Him there. When G-d sent His only begotten Son into the World, He was, essentially, returning, the only environment where you are able to *function in your true authentic self*, in relation to Him. The Father seeks to have an encounter with you, on His turf.

g. MAKING A MENTAL ALIYAH

The P'ne-El Therapy Book aims to give you the support you need to make the *mental Aliyah*, necessary to elevate your mind, will and emotions to that higher place in G-d. You are

---

[93] B'resheet 2: 7, 8

required to **step up to that place of intimacy with G-d** because He so desires it.

> [8] "For my thoughts are not your thoughts, and your ways are not my ways," says *ADONAI.* [9] "As high as the sky is above the earth are my ways higher than your ways, and my thoughts than your thoughts ..."

Yesha'yahu 55: 8, 9

h. IDENTIFY YOUR SYMTOMS

This in-depth therapeutic course will help you to measure your spiritual condition. It will cause hidden faults in your life to come to the surface or even make you feel **unsettled**. This course of study may cause the reopening of old wounds and show that **treatment** is the necessary **next-step**. A prescribed course of action will be the recommended solution.

If you were not aware of **how to** identify your symptoms, at the start of this course, you will become well aware of what they are by the time you have finished reading this book. The hidden strangers within, are likely to *make you feel defensive*. **Defensiveness to the Truth**, highlights the presence of demonic control. **The challenge for you**, will be to *acknowledge* the symptoms which have surfaced, *isolate* them and *repent*. This action **cannot be done without the right level of supervision.**

i.   THE FIRST STEP TOWARDS LIBERATION

In this process of liberation, you must **acknowledge and repent for your own sins**; the sins you chose to commit. Take an in-depth self-inventory and repent to G-d for every area where there is unrepentant sin in your life.

j.   THE SECOND STEP TOWARDS LIBERATION

In this process of your liberation, you must identify the generational sins and iniquities that are at work in your family. **A critical analysis of your relatives**, will determine the nature of the familial spirits attached to your bloodline.

k.   THE THIRD STEP TOWARDS LIBERATION

In this process of liberation, **you must forgive your ancestors for opening the door** to sin in your family line. "If you forgive someone's sin, their sins are forgiven; if you hold them, they are held."[94] The **power of our ancestor's sin will not be broken over our lives unless we forgive them.**[95] Unforgiveness will cause demonic forces to maintain their power over our lives. Be vigilant and do not allow bitterness or anger in your heart against those who initiated or perpetrated bondages in your family line.

---

[94] Yochanan 20: 23
[95] Nechemyah (Nehemiah) 9: 2

---

l. THE FOURTH STEP TOWARDS LIBERATION

In this process of liberation, you must repent for the sins in
your own generation. Since you are *a living relative*, you have
the authority to ask G-d to forgive the sins caused by a
person or persons in your generational bloodline. You can
appropriate the blood of *Yeshua HaMashiach* in your
bloodline, where that sin has been committed and **break the
power** of that sin back to ten generations on both sides of
your family.

m. CONCLUSION

Call out those hidden strangers in your bloodline, by name.
Renounce the sin related to you and **command them to
leave and never return**. By doing this, you will **remove
Hasatan's legal right to continue tormenting you and your
children** in that area. Understanding generational sin and
iniquity, and how to break free from it, is one of the major
keys to possessing your inheritance.

12 *Calling Leaders to Freedom*

This short chapter seeks to encourage all leaders to take accountability for their own liberation. Leaders carry great influence therefore, they must first undergo liberation before they can be instrumental in liberating those whom they lead. Moshe needed to be free from the shackles of life in the household of Egypt's Pharaoh.[96] He saw the misery of a slave population to which he was related.

Though he grew up in Pharaoh's palace, he was nevertheless, directly related to a *four- hundred-year* slave population. G-d called Moshe to deliver his people from slavery, however, Moshe needed to be alone with G-d, and separated from the stench of slavery, in order to experience freedom. In fact, Moshe's preparation to become the deliverer of his people, is a prime example of what is required of every leader.

a. SELF DIAGNOSIS AND PROGNOSIS SHEET

Leaders must prayerfully go through the **'Self-diagnosis and prognosis sheet'** provided in the Book entitled, *The Seven Enemies of the Soul*, by Dr Beverley M. Anderson. Time

---

[96] Messianic Jews 11:27

---

spent alone with your 'Self Diagnosis and Prognosis Sheet,' will help you to identify and acknowledge your own sins and the sins in your generational and ancestral lineage, in an organized fashion. As **a prophetic act**, you will be required to sign your 'Self Diagnosis and Prognosis Sheet' on completion, after which it will be burned.

b. WEAKNESS AWARENESS SHEET

A second sheet provided, will allow you to be aware of the weaknesses in your own bloodline and itemize them as a reminder of **how to** take preventative measures.

c. PRAYER OF REPENTANCE SHEET

The Prayer of Repentance Sheet, will provide leaders with prayers that are based on G-d's Word. They will include:

1. Sins you committed in your past.

2. Sins brought to mind that you forgot about.

3. Family sins that you know about.

4. Generational sins

5. Ministerial Sins

6. Sins against the Jews

d. THE PROPHETIC ACT

After you have completed the **Prayer of Repentance Sheet**, it must be completely burned up as *a prophetic act* and sign that you have secured your liberation from past sins.

e. PRAYER OF PROTECTION SHEET

A **Prayer of Protection Sheet** will be provided in Book Two, entitled: 'The Seven Enemies of the Soul.' Whilst praying, *you will be advised to anointed your head with oil* as a symbol of the *Ruach HaKodesh* covering. Alternatively, if as a leader, you feel a little apprehensive about going through **the renunciation** process alone, I strongly advise you to look for support from those who have spiritual accountability over you. Failing this, try to find two or three leaders who will stand with you during this process.

f. RENUNCIATIONS: THE SEVEN ENEMIES OF KENA'AN

The lists of renunciations in Book Two are divided into seven categories. Start the renunciation process from the beginning and work your way to the end. It will take between one to two hours from start to finish. Alternatively, each of the seven sections can be spread over seven weeks. Make sure that each renunciation is **clear, firm** and **convincing**. When evil spirits exit, some of you may feel the urge to vomit, some may start to cough, others will feel like yawning

g. THE TREATMENT APPLICATION SHEET

Your Treatment Application Sheet is a daily confessional. It is based on a list of Scriptural Bible Texts. Be accountable to anointed leaders who have had years of wisdom behind them and who are committed to seeing that you are creating new habits based on your confession of G-d's Word. The daily Scriptural Confessions will help you to agree with who the Word says you are. Knowing your identity in the Messiah is the key to being an overcomer in this World.

h. CONCLUSION

In conclusion, it is advised that all who sit under this teaching, must seek continued counsel and spiritual support. You may need to read this book several times before going on to Book Two. Don't be surprized at the reaction this teaching course will arouse in you. In my own ministerial experiences, I have witnessed *hidden strangers* come to the surface and put up a fight simply because they were confronted by the truth. In many instances, the person being liberated had no idea that they were carriers of such a fierce resistance.

I can't stop you from purchasing this course, however, I strongly advise you to **take counsel before embarking on Book Two**. Remember, as a third generational relative, Ya'akov was called to close the door on generational sin and iniquity in his bloodline. As he thought about facing his twin brother Esav (Esau), he began to experience a fear that wasn't his. He understood that he needed to first *confront the hidden strangers in his bloodline* before confronting his brother. Ya'akov made a firm decision to hold on to **the Angel of the L-rd** and confront his issues, in order to, overcome that spiritual hurdle. His *perseverance resulted in a breakthrough for his family and his descendants.* When he eventually met Esav, the encounter was *peaceful.* Though Ya'akov experienced some symptoms of fear, prior to meeting his twin brother, he was no longer captive to the spirit of fear.

[18] After consultation, plans succeed; so take wise advice when waging war.

Mishlei (Proverbs) 20: 18

Glossary

DNA – Deoxyribonucleic acid or DNA is a molecule that contains the instructions an organism needs to develop, life and reproduce. These instructions are found inside every cell, and are passed down from parents to their children.

A person's DNA contains information about their heritage, and can sometimes reveal whether they are at risk for certain diseases. DNA tests, genetic tests, are used for a variety of reasons, including to diagnose genetic disorders, to determine whether a person is a carrier of a genetic mutation that they could pass on to their children, and to examine whether a person is at risk for genetic disease

El 'Elyon – G-d Most High

Esav - Esau

HaMashiach – 'The Messiah

Hasatan (Satan) – Literally, "the Adversary."

Kasdim – Chaldeans (modern day Iraq)

K'ruv, k'ruvim (cherub, cherubim) – Heavenly creatures (angels) who guarded the way to the Tree of Life in Gan-

'Eden (Gen. 3:24), were described by Ezekiel as having four faces and four wings (Ezek. 10:20-21), and were ridden by G-d (Ps. 18:11 [10]); compare the "living beings" of Rev. 4:6ff. The term also refers to the gold overlaid wooden images of the same, constructed in obedience to G-d's command, which overshadowed the ark of the covenant in the tabernacle and in the Temple. Heb. 9:5.

Kena'an – Canaan

Mitzvah, pl. *Mitzvot* – literally; "command," "commandment"; more broadly: general principle for living, good deed. Mt 5: 19+

Moshe (Moses) – (1) Deliverer of Isra'el from Egypt, agent through whom Isra'el received the *Torah*. Matt. 8:4. (2) In the time of Yeshua and after, the "seat of Moshe" was not only a metaphor for the authority of the *Torah*-teachers but an actual chair on which they sat when they taught. Matt. 23:2.

Mutual Imprecations – Originally from a Latin word meaning to 'invoke evil" or bring down bad spirits upon." Not to be confused with *implication,* a similar sounding word with the completely unrelated meaning of implying something directly. An imprecation is a type of condemnation, curse or execration. It is an appeal to some supernatural power to inflict evil on someone or some group.[97]

New Birth Experience – this refers to a spiritual rebirth or the new life a person finds when he or she becomes a believer in ADONAI, Yeshua HaMashiach. This concept is also referred to as "salvation," "regeneration," or being born again."[98]

'olam hazeh – This world, this age. Matt. 12:32.

Rivkah - Rebecca

Ruach HaKodesh – the Holy Spirit, referred to four times in the Tanakh as such, and many times as the Spirit of G-d. Mt 1: 18+

Talmid – fem. *talmidah*, pl. *talmidim* – disciple, student. The relationship between a talmid and his rabbi was very close: not only did the *talmid* learn facts, reasoning processes and how to perform religious practices from his rabbi, but he regarded him as an example to be imitated in conduct and character (see Mt 10:24-25; Lk 6:40; Yn 13:13-15;1C 11:1). The rabbi, in turn, was considered responsible for his talmidim (Mt 12:2; Lk 19:39; Yn 17:12;). Mt 5:1+.

---

[97] https://www.vocabulary.com/dictionary/imprecation
[98] https://www.gotquestions.org/spiritual-rebirth.html

Teraphim – **(1)** The word *Teraphim* is explained in classical rabbinical literature as meaning disgraceful things. That Micah, who worshipped Yahweh, used the *Teraphim* as an idol, and that Laban regarded the *Teraphim* as representing his gods, is thought to indicate that they were evidently images of Yahweh. It is considered possible that they originated as a fetish, possibly initially representative of ancestors, but gradually becoming oracular.[99]

(2) Family gods or idols, at times consulted for omens (Yechezk'el 21:21) Some were the size and shape of a man, while others were much smaller. (B'resheet 31:34; Sh'mu'el Alef 19:13,16) Archaeological findings in Mesopotamia indicate that possessing the teraphim images had a bearing on who would receive the family inheritance. (This may explain why Rachel took her father's teraphim.)[100]

Torah – Literally, "teaching," but usually translated "law" because Greek uses *nomos* ("law") to render Hebrew *Torah*. (1) The Five Books of Moses, the Pentateuch (Genesis, Exodus, Leviticus, Numbers and Deuteronomy), called the written *Torah*. Matt. 5:17. (2) That, plus the *Nevi'im* (Prophets) and *K'tuvim* (Writings), i.e., the whole *Tanakh*. John 10: 34. (3) That, plus additional material (Oral *Torah*) considered in varying degree authoritative in Judaism. Gal. 5: 3. (4)

---

[99] https://en.m.wikipedia.org/wiki/Teraphim
[100] https://www.jw.org/en/publications/books/bible-glossary/teraphim/

Uncapitalized, *torah* can be understood generically as "law" or "principle." Rom. 7: 21 – 8: 2.

Ya'akov - Jacob

Yitz'chak – Isaac

Y'hudah - Judah[101]

---

[101] Glossary of Hebrew words taken from *The Complete Jewish Bible*, updated edition, 2016

Author's Contact Details

Email: bm.rose.anderson@gmail.com

Facebook:
https://www.facebook.com/drbeverleyanderson/